BE YOUR OWN BRAND

BE YOUR OWN BRAND

A Breakthrough Formula
for Standing Out from the Crowd

David McNally and Karl D. Speak

BERRETT-KOEHLER PUBLISHERS, INC.
San Francisco

Berrett-Koehler Publishers, Inc.
235 Montgomery Street, Suite 650
San Francisco, CA 94104-2916
Tel: (415) 288-0260 / Fax: (415) 362-2512
www.bkconnection.com

Ordering Information

Quantity sales. Special discounts are available on quantity purchases by corporations, associations, and others. For details, contact the "Special Sales Department" at the Berrett-Koehler address above.

Individual sales. Berrett-Koehler publications are available through most bookstores. They can also be ordered direct from Berrett-Koehler: Tel: (800) 929-2929; Fax: (802) 864-7626; www.bkconnection.com

Orders for college textbook/course adoption use. Please contact Berrett-Koehler: Tel: (800) 929-2929; Fax: (802) 864-7626.

Orders by U.S. trade bookstores and wholesalers. Please contact Publishers Group West, 1700 Fourth Street, Berkeley, CA 94710. Tel: (510) 528-1444; Fax (510) 528-3444.

Printed in the United States of America

Berrett-Koehler books are printed on long-lasting acid-free paper. When it is available, we choose paper that has been manufactured by environmentally responsible processes. These may include using trees grown in sustainable forests, incorporating recycled paper, minimizing chlorine in bleaching, or recycling the energy produced at the paper mill.

Library of Congress Cataloging-in-Publication Data
McNally, David, 1946-
    Be your own brand : a breakthrough formula for standing out from the crowd / by David McNally & Karl D. Speak.
        p.   cm.
    Includes bibliographical references and index.
    ISBN-10: 1-57675-141-4; ISBN-13: 978-1-57675-141-1
    ISBN-10: 1-57675-272-0; ISBN-13: 978-1-57675-272-2 (pbk.)
    1. Identity (Psychology) 2. Brand name products—Miscellanea.
I. Speak, Karl D., 1951- II. title.
BF697 .M385   2001
158'.1—dc21   2001043852

First Edition
09 08 07 06   10 9 8 7 6 5 4

Project management, design, and composition: BookMatters, Berkeley; Copyedit: Deborah Notkin; Proofreading: Ann Foley; Index: Ken DellaPenta

Contents

ACKNOWLEDGMENTS   vii

FOREWORD   ix

1   Personal Branding   1
Becoming More of Who You Are

2   Personal Brand Characteristics   13
Distinctive, Relevant, and Consistent

3   Personal Brand Dimensions   25
Roles, Standards, and Style

4   Personal Brand Authenticity   45
Purpose, Vision, and Values

5   Personal Brand Framework   59
Defining Your Unique Brand

6   Personal Brand Promise   73
Making a Commitment to Your Brand

7   Personal Brand Strategies   87
Measuring and Strengthening Your Brand

8   Sign Up or Sign Out   101
Aligning with Your Employer's Brand

9   The Courage to Live Your Brand   117

APPENDIX I: BRAND VALUES PROFILE   129

APPENDIX II: PERSONAL BRAND MANIFESTOS   131

APPENDIX III: READING LIST   139

INDEX   141

Acknowledgments

I have learned a great deal in the writing of this book. My coauthor, Karl Speak, is unquestionably a leading authority on the art and science of building strong brands. I continue to benefit significantly, both personally and professionally, from his contribution to this work. My wife, Jo, tirelessly demonstrates her faith in me. My children, Sarah, Kate, Sean, Jessie, and Beth, ensure that my life will never be dull. My assistant, Jo Reinhart, is a rock of stability in any storm. And there are those who generously gave their time to read and comment on the manuscript: Mike Boland, Rebecca Bradshaw, Fritz Corrigan, Kevin Dillon, Jim Gabbert, Mark Moore, Judy Pennington, Bill Rutherford, Neil Schermitzler, and Pat Schreiber.

You all, unquestionably, stand out from the crowd.

David McNally

I had high expectations for writing my first book. I envisioned it would be a fun, intense, and exhilarating experience. It met all my expectations, plus more. The one surprise in the whole process was the important role my family, friends, and colleagues would play in this fascinating experience. Without a doubt the person on the top of my list is my wife, Beth. Her continual support and "Steady-Eddie" personality will always be a prime source of energy for me. My sweet daughter Kathryn ("right, wrong, but never in doubt") is a major source of inspiration for me, this book included. John Williamson provided me the inspiration to take the concept of brands and make it personal. His spirit was profound and will have an everlasting impact on me. Ron Mogel on the other hand made my understanding of brands as a business tool richer and added to my yearning to learn even more about them. My coauthor David McNally continues to share the wisdom of a seasoned author. The following people provided important feedback on the draft of the manuscript: Jim Nygard, Barbara Kelly, Beth Speak, Jacque Rast, Marianne Richmond, Jen Williams, Becky Ewert, Steve Hanson, Dan Yaman, James Scothorn and Dave Cieslak. And last, but not least, I want to acknowledge my mother for providing me unceasing encouragement with her most poignant observation—"This book seems like a lot of extra work for you; I hope it's worth it." Don't worry, Mom, it was.

Karl D. Speak

Together we would like to acknowledge Dick Schaaf for his insights and hard work to synthesize our ideas and words into a cogent text. There is no doubt that this book would still be a work-in-progress without his expertise and professionalism.

Foreword

When David McNally and Karl Speak approached me to help them research and produce the book you now hold, I admit to being skeptical. At first, it seemed a mix of viewpoints and styles at odds with each other—David's expertise in motivation and personal development, as evidenced by his bestselling books *Even Eagles Need a Push* and *The Eagle's Secret,* and Karl's hard-driving business edge, resulting from his work as a brand development consultant to organizations such as Cargill, FedEx, Target, and *The Wall Street Journal.*

One guy soars. The other guy digs. One speaks to the unquantifiable elements of human potential. The other focuses on very tangible aspects of business performance. And yet, who better to approach the tantalizing prospect of using business wisdom to create personal success than two very different experts who, between them, cover all points on the spectrum?

As people of all ages and backgrounds struggle to come to terms with a world where little appears solid or constant, the idea of personal branding has become more and more intriguing. The importance of brands in building and sustaining corporate success is well documented. A brand is a reflection of the relationship an organization has with its customers, embodying that which an organization is committed to and stands for.

David and Karl believe that for individuals to succeed in an ever more competitive and complex world, they need to be diligent about building the strength of their own *personal* brand. In other words, what are we committed to, what do we stand for, and, more critically, how do we represent that to the outside world? As people cannot see inside of us, the recognition of our beliefs and abilities can only come from what people see us do, the perception they form from observing our day-to-day actions. Through our actions, therefore, we build our *brand*.

What David and Karl will show you in the pages that follow is elegantly simple, yet highly sophisticated. They present a formula that combines a number of different elements—some from the business world, some from more personal dimensions—into a larger whole. Their purpose is to help the reader not only identify and establish his or her unique place in the world but also benefit from the recognition of their individuality.

To help you in your process, *Be Your Own Brand* leaves out the celebrities and focuses on examples of people you've never heard of but who exemplify what it means to have a strong personal brand: a trainer from Texas and a heart surgeon from Minneapolis; a California-based financial advisor and an icon of Canadian national pride; a fashion-trend spotter with a flair for making large systems turn tight corners and an ex-hippie whose hair may be shorter, but whose gentle spirit has not been suppressed by the world of corporate cubicles.

These are people who have figured out how to *be* their own brand. They have found a way to break through the noise and clutter of modern life to give a clear impression of who they really are, what they value, and how they can be counted upon to act. They clearly stand out from the crowd.

What they can do, you can do, too. David and Karl are about to show you how.

Dick Schaaf

1 **Personal Branding**

Becoming More of Who You Are

Ever get the feeling that people—even people who know you (or should know you) very well—just don't "get" you? That they don't quite understand who you really are and what they can rely on you to do for them?

Ever get the feeling that the relationships in your life—some of them, anyway—are a little out of sync with your ideals and what you really want? That you're being forced to make choices, some of them uncomfortable, between who you know yourself to be and who someone else wants you to be?

Ever get the feeling that there's a troubling disconnect—maybe only minor, maybe profound—between your personal life and your professional life? That the demands of your job, your career, your business, are in conflict with your values?

In every case described above, there seems to be a gap between perception and reality, between the "real you" and the you other people see and interact with. At work, at home, in the community, in life in general, you're not getting as much credit as you think you should for who you really are and what you really believe. Somehow, it's as though you are being asked—even compelled—to be less of yourself rather than more.

Businesses deal with this dilemma constantly. Their most successful responses tend to focus on one key concept—**brand.**

- Brand is how businesses tell customers what to expect. Things can change rapidly in the business world, and customers are more comfortable if they know what to expect.
- Brand is a familiar bridge across which businesses and their customers conduct transactions that lead to long-term and mutually beneficial relationships.
- Brand is the embodiment of what businesses and their customers value, the means through which businesses get credit for the quality they represent and deliver.

We think successful people can do what successful businesses do. The principles businesses use to "teach" their customers what to expect from their products and services can have powerful applications in both our personal and our professional lives.

From our more than twenty years in the business world, we know these principles, and we've developed techniques based on them—techniques that work. Our "day jobs" involve helping businesses with just these kinds of issues. More importantly, we've discovered that these same principles apply far beyond the world of business. Best of all, we know you don't need an MBA to understand and apply these ideas. In the pages that follow, we'll show you how to conceive, convey, and manage a strong brand—an accurate reflection of who you *really* are—in ways that will help you define and meet the expectations of the important people in your life. We'll use business examples for illustration, but we won't overdo arcane science. We'll keep it short. We'll keep it simple. We'll keep it easy to apply in your own life.

What Exactly *Is* a Brand?

A brand is a relationship. It is not a statement. It is not a matter of contrived image, or colorful packaging, or snappy slogans, or adding an artificial veneer to disguise the true nature of what's within. In fact, a "branded" relationship is a special type of relationship—one that involves the kind of trust that only happens when two people believe there is a direct connection between their value systems.

Success is not something the world can define for you. It's what *you* define it to be, based on *your* particular values and aspirations.

If those two basic premises make sense to you, there is an excellent chance that what follows will dramatically transform, for the better, the understanding you have of yourself and the relationships you have with the important people in your life: at home, at work, in all of the various communities to which you belong.

Dealing with issues that involve values can be a delicate matter. The word "values" has personal connotations in both the moral and the material worlds, and we have no ambition to take a stand in a pulpit, bully or otherwise. Yet, frankly, there's no other way to show you how to successfully build a personal brand than to connect it to your values.

Similarly, dealing with personal issues in conjunction with a powerful (and often misunderstood) concept from the business world can be equally dicey. Like "values," the word "brand" is often misused, its true meaning lost in the technical stew of logos and product offerings and ad campaigns and marketing slogans.

We've put the information into an orderly structure (so you know what to expect). We're going to deal with brand and values in each context—business and personal—separately. Then we'll show you how to connect them in ways that can have a profound impact on your personal and professional life. You know a lot of this already. You've probably just never considered it in the context of a brand. You will.

- First, we'll define what we mean by brand and show you how, in business, a strong brand is systematically built and managed.

- Second, we'll show you the far-reaching personal applications of these brand-management fundamentals.
- Third, we'll offer more depth and detail on how businesses evolve their brands while making sure they remain true to their core mission.
- Finally, we'll show you how these advanced brand-management techniques apply to your own personal and professional relationships.

Brand Basics

In business, the concept of brand has a well-defined meaning:

A brand is a perception or emotion, maintained by a buyer or a prospective buyer, describing the experience related to doing business with an organization or consuming its products or services.

To put the idea of brand in a personal context, think of it this way:

Your brand is a perception or emotion, maintained by somebody other than you, that describes the total experience of having a relationship with you.

Everybody already has a brand. Your brand is a reflection of who you are and what you believe, which is visibly expressed by what you do and how you do it. It's the doing part that connects you with someone else, and that connection with someone else results in a relationship. In reality, the image of your brand is a perception held in someone else's mind. As that perception, through repeated contacts between you and the other person, evolves and sharpens, a brand relationship takes form.

The key to the concept, whether business or personal, is to understand the nature and needs of a relationship. Business success is seldom an accident, any more than personal success in life results from some cosmic coincidence. Nor can either form of success be achieved in isolation. Both hinge on the success or failure of relationships.

In business, the principles and techniques of brand management allow organizations to focus on strategies and tactics that build strong relationships. The success of those relationships helps the business's products and services—and, behind those, the people who form the business—achieve an overall set of objectives. But this only works when the relationships meet the real needs of the people with whom those organizations do business: customers, shareholders, other stakeholders, employees, and the community at large.

Finding a "bottom line" for personal success is less clear-cut. The individual values and objectives of people are so varied. But no matter what your vision of life may be, the most critical component of your ultimate success or failure is the breadth and depth of your relationships. You want your family, your friends, your employer, and your coworkers to truly understand and fully acknowledge who you are and what you do. That's what will make those relationships mutually enjoyable and valuable. That's the essence of a "branded" relationship.

A branded relationship is a special one—in many ways, the most loyal kind of relationship there is. Many of the proven, successful loyalty-building ideas and tactics used by businesses in managing their brands can be brought to bear on your own personal relationships, with outstanding results. As you learn to understand and apply sensible, practical brand-development and self-management principles, you will gain tools you can use to create and progressively strengthen your relationships with the people you interact with on a regular basis.

By developing a strong personal brand that is clear, complete, and valuable to others, you will create a life that is much more successful and fulfilling. They win. You win. That's the kind of success that can have far-reaching benefits.

The Images Between

What does a personal brand, strong or otherwise, look like? How will people know it when they see it? Think for a moment of someone you know well professionally. How would you describe your relationship with that person? Is this someone with whom you can easily discuss a problem, or someone you'd probably avoid in a sensitive situation? Do you think of them first when you need help or expertise in a particular area, or last? Why does this individual stand out among the hundreds of people in your mental address book?

That is your brand perception of them—a reflection of who you believe them to be, based at least in part on what you think their values are. Their brand exists in your mind (just as your brand exists in theirs) based on who you've known them to be and what you've known them to do. It's how you judge them now and how you know what to expect from them the next time you interact. It may or may not be a perception they've consciously worked to create in your mind . . . but that's getting a little ahead of our story.

Now think of someone you know well on a personal level. How would you describe your relationship with that person? Again, is this someone in whom you can confide? Someone to turn to in times of trouble? Or someone to steer clear of when the chips are down? Why does this person have a special place in your thoughts and affections? All these perceptions reflect a personal equivalent of the same brand relationships we've learned to recognize and resonate with in business.

Quality and Quantity

Personal or corporate, brands are all around us—so much so that we often look right past them or take them for granted. Some brand experts say that strong brands can "hide in plain sight." In other words, when a brand is really, really good we take it for granted, just as we can take for granted those people who are very important in our lives, and yet we rarely take the time to consider why.

Whether we're aware of them or not, however, brands have tremendous power in our world.

- It's estimated that the average person in North America is exposed to more than three thousand brand messages each and every day.
- Across all categories, research shows people are willing to pay nine to twelve percent higher prices on average for a brand they know and trust compared to brands with which they may not be as familiar.
- Coca-Cola's brand is estimated to be worth about half the company's total market value.

Business considerations aside, however, what comes to mind when you think of the word "brand"? A color? A shape? A price? Maybe. But probably not. Instead, when you think about brands, chances are you think about whether you *trust* them or not, *like* them or not, *remember* them or not, *value* them or not.

Over the past two decades, when researchers have asked consumers what values they associate with brands, the number one answer is some variation on quality. Not quantity. Quality. And if you look for the dominant element in words like "trust" and "like" and "remember" and "value," you'll find it's a feeling, a strong emotional component.

Relationships have at their heart emotions—intangible attributes, not measurable ones. In the relationships that matter in your life, which rules, the head or the heart?

The heart, of course. When we flip the relationship coin, hearts invariably beat heads. Ideally, the emotions we feel (what our hearts are telling us) align closely with more objective measures (what our heads are telling us). But not always. Sometimes, in fact, the heart defies the head and we cling to feelings, positive or negative, that defy rational analysis. That doesn't make those feelings any less real, or us weird. It makes us human.

Consequently, for people to relate strongly to our personal brand, their hearts as well as their heads have to be involved. And the more positive both the quality and the quantity measurements turn out to be, the stronger the relationship will turn out to be.

In life, as in business, the relationships that have the greatest value and staying power are the ones where positive emotions predominate. The relationships between parents and children, spouses, very close friends, and long-time mentors and protégés are by definition much stronger than those between casual acquaintances. The emotional content is the difference. And it shows.

Think about the most important relationships in your life, and you'll come up with senses or feelings—emotions. When you think of your spouse, your children, your parents, or your closest friends, there's as much emotional kick in the mental image as there is in the simple objective label: "Oh, that's my dad, my mom, the love of my life, my kids, or my best buddy from college or the Navy or the team at work." Special relationships have emotions tied to them. That's what makes them so special.

Small wonder that really great brands, whether personal or product, transcend the quantifiable to conjure up powerful emotions, especially positive emotions. When a business brand achieves that status, it has real power. And when a personal brand builds similar linkages to the heart as well as the head, it too has real power.

Try this: If your best friend, spouse, or partner were a brand, what brand would they be and why? Conversely, if they were asked to describe you as a brand, what images would they come up with? Are you a Honda (efficient, reliable, functional) or a Maserati (exciting, exotic, spontaneous)? A Ritz-Carlton (high-amenity, attentive, elegant) or a Motel 6 (simple, unpretentious, efficient)? A Harvard (intellectual, demanding, teaching professional skills) or a KinderCare (safe, nurturing, teaching formative skills)?

Each is a strong, valuable brand. Each can be the appropriate brand for a given set of circumstances, yet an inappropriate brand in other contexts. Whether it's right depends on the needs of the relationship, not the intrinsic nature of the product or service. You wouldn't send your high-achieving teenager to KinderCare or your four year old to Harvard. You can sleep like a baby at a Ritz-Carlton or a Motel 6, but your choice between the two may depend on whether you have a tight budget or a lavish expense account. Both a Honda and a Maserati have four tires, seats, and a steering wheel—and both can be satisfying to drive—but which one you want depends on whether you're going to a Grand Prix or the grocery store.

One *Really* Nice Guy

For Karl, a good example of a strong personal brand is Dr. Chip R. Bell. He's an author, a trainer, and a consultant. He has a well-developed sense of humor, an engaging Southern drawl, and a depth of expertise that extends from customer service to leadership and the protocols of great partnerships. But most importantly in this context, Chip Bell is a nice guy.

"So what?" you may say. The world is full of nice guys. Big deal.

No, Chip Bell is a *nice* guy. Chip Bell embodies an off-the-chart exuberance for life. To anyone who has come within the gravitational pull of his personality, he is the poster boy for contagious enthusiasm. Chip Bell radiates an active, assertive, outgoing friendliness into a room. A couple of years ago, he and Karl partnered on a consulting road trip in the Pacific Northwest, and Karl still clearly recalls witnessing dimensions of enthusiasm he had never suspected existed.

By his actions and example, Chip Bell inspired Karl—and undoubtedly a lot of other people—to take the personal brand component of optimism and enthusiasm to a whole new level. People do that to us periodically. They take something we believe is one of our own greatest strengths and redefine it right before our eyes, simultaneously transforming it and us.

But what makes Chip Bell such an extraordinary example of a strong personal brand to Karl is the sheer genuineness of his behavior, from the moment he greets you to the moment you part. When you look into Chip Bell's eyes, he's completely there. In that moment, the connection he makes has a power and a relevance that transcends anything else that's going on in the room.

Did Chip Bell set out to be the nicest, most enthusiastic guy on the planet? Not at all. He's not engaged in a competitive endeavor. Nor is it a function of his actions alone. Rather, Chip Bell *values* friendliness—values it extremely highly—and that, in turn, dictates his outgoing, involved behavior.

It's an amazing thing to stand next to and watch Chip Bell. There's no self-consciousness. No sense of pretense or artifice. In other words, Chip Bell's **authenticity** (a word we'll come back to at some length later) is so apparent that the impact it has on others is immediate and lasting.

Your values and habits may not be the same as Chip Bell's. Nor should they be, if his brand doesn't contribute to an accurate reflection of who *you* are. But when you can indelibly imprint yourself on the mind of someone else, you've arrived as a strong personal brand.

The Power of Two (and More)

So far, what have we established?

That brands are valuable to businesses. That relationships turn on their emotional content. That actions spring from and tie back to values. And that somebody named Chip Bell is a really nice guy.

Most importantly, we hope you can now clearly see that a brand reflects a perception or emotion maintained *in somebody else's mind.* This is an area where perception is reality. It doesn't matter nearly as much what you think. It matters a whole lot what *other people* think. Your brand, just like the brand of a product, exists on the basis of a set of perceptions and emotions stored in someone else's head.

The good news about a perception or emotion is that once locked in place, it has tremendous staying power. Just as highly personalized perceptions and emotions stick with a product, they stick with a person. Their staying power is what gives a relationship its resilience. Once people accept the basic values of a brand, they judge their subsequent experiences with it against that norm—they interpret the actions they experience or observe in the context of the values they believe to be at the heart of the brand.

- If you make a mistake or fall short of fulfilling a promise occasionally, the previous reliability of your strong personal brand is there to reassure people. They'll discount the out-of-kilter action as a one-time exception, an aberration, because they trust that the underlying values are still in place. (Of course, fall short on a regular basis and people will undoubtedly begin to revise their value assessments.)

- When you go above and beyond someone's expectations, on the other hand, the brand relationship becomes even stronger and more cherished. The values people believe are at work below the surface magnify the effects of the actions, with corresponding effects on the depth and strength of the relationship. Again, the more often that happens, the greater the impact.

Building a personal brand is a lot more than a weekend project. For all of the talk about first impressions, brand strength actually comes from repeated impressions — impressions that, as we'll see in the next chapter, clearly stand out in the specific context of the relationship.

Getting Down to Business

What's the primary benefit to *you* of developing a strong personal brand? We think it's that you get to be more of who and what you are, not less. In other words, you get to live your values—to be acknowledged and receive credit not only for what you do but also for what you believe. You end up, therefore, feeling a whole lot better about life in general because—in essence and in fact—you are being true to yourself. That, to us, is the essence of personal success.

Building a strong personal brand can be very challenging, especially when you begin to apply brand-management principles in a world where so many different kinds of relationships define our lives.

In the next two chapters, we'll take a detailed look at the art of branding in modern business, with some initial observations on how to apply these principles on a personal basis. In the chapters that follow, we'll use the wisdom of the business form of branding to illustrate what makes *people* memorable, indispensable, invaluable, trusted, and desired—what happens when their actions connect back to their inner values. From this foundation, we'll then show you how you can use advanced branding techniques from the world of business to take your own personal brand to a much higher level with the people who matter most to you.

2 | **Personal Brand Characteristics**

Distinctive, Relevant, and Consistent

To make personal branding work for you, you need to understand how a business brand works. The principles and ideas developed and successfully used in business over many years are readily adaptable to building a personal brand.

For starters, since your brand is a perception maintained in someone else's mind, how others see you is the central issue. A strong brand, corporate or personal, needs to be so clearly defined that its intended audience can quickly grasp what it stands for. For a business, the audience is its customers. For a personal brand, it is those with whom we have (or want to have) relationships.

Three key components combine to determine the strength of a brand. Strong brands are

- **Distinctive:** they stand for something. They have a point of view.
- **Relevant:** what they stand for connects to what someone else considers to be important.
- **Consistent:** people come to believe in a relationship based on the consistency of behaviors they experience or observe.

In Chapter 1, we discussed how a brand is a relationship and how that relationship develops from emotional connections. You make and maintain those emotional connections by being distinctive, relevant, and consistent. In other words, when your actions are distinctive, relevant, and consistent, your intended audience begins to see and understand your brand.

Let's examine how the application of each component affects the relationships in your life.

Strong Personal Brands Are Distinctive

Your brand starts to become *strong* when you decide what you believe in and then *commit* yourself to acting on those beliefs. At that very point, you begin to separate yourself from the crowd. Here's why: Making a commitment means doing what you said you would do despite the obstacles. As your beliefs are not always shared by another, standing up for and holding to them is often a courageous act, and courage of this kind is none too common in our world. That, by definition, is distinctive.

To truly understand what it means to be distinctive is to learn that it implies much more than just being different. Brand building is not image building. It is not selling yourself to someone else. It results from understanding the needs of others, wanting to meet those needs, and being able to do so while staying true to your values.

As we'll see in greater detail in Chapter 4, clarifying, understanding, and acting on the basis of values is a core building block in the art of developing a strong personal brand. For now, suffice it to say that your values are the beliefs you hold to be true, the principles by which you live your life. They include what you're interested in and what you're committed to. They influence how you prioritize competing demands.

Your values affect not only what you think and feel but also how you behave. In fact, how you act on your values distinguishes you from the crowd. As people observe your actions, they make judgments about why you do what you do. Those judgments then become the perception of you they carry around with them. The more distinctive the actions they see, the better defined your brand becomes for them. In other words, personal brands connect and grow strong when they focus on meeting the needs of others without sacrificing the values on which they are based.

We cannot emphasize enough, therefore, that a strong personal brand is not some kind of veneer—something painted on to present a more pleasing appearance. It is a reflection of those ideas and values that are distinctively you. This is the only substance upon which a truly lasting relationship can be built. The lesson:

Your personal brand is based on your values, not the other way around.

Strong Personal Brands Are Relevant

Being distinctive is not the only thing that matters to someone else. What you stand for needs to be relevant to them. Relevance begins when a person believes that you understand and care about what's important to them. It gains strength every time you demonstrate that what's important to them is important to you. The synergistic effect of being both distinctive and relevant is what ignites the power of a personal brand.

Relevance is often a function of circumstances. Parents are naturally relevant to their children, for they are the caregivers and protectors of those children. The relevance of one spouse to another extends far beyond the bonds of a marriage contract: the actual relevance occurs when both people in the marriage are concerned about and committed to each other's well-being.

Relevance is what distinguishes a friend from an acquaintance. A coworker may be only relevant to the degree that what they do affects what you do, whereas a mentor's support and interest in your career and future makes that relationship far more valued and lasting than an ordinary relationship with a fellow employee. Your relevance to a client or customer is determined not only by your product or service but by how it (and you) can proficiently solve their problems and meet their needs. The more relevance you demonstrate, the stronger your brand becomes to them. That is why strong brands always attract attention: they attract the most attention from those who find them the most relevant.

Building relevance involves a skill we call "thinking in reverse." If you want to be considered valuable to others, you must move out of your world into theirs. Your first concern is to determine their needs and interests. Then you have to connect those needs and interests to your own personal strengths and abilities. The sages throughout the ages have said in many different ways: "Before you can get what *you* want, you must first help others get what *they* want."

That means relevance is a process. It starts with questions. What do *they* want? What do *they* need? What do *they* value? What do *they* expect? When you have a sense of someone else's needs and their frame of reference, that information allows you to guide your actions in ways that will make you relevant. Which leads us to the fact that there is a strong aspirational element involved in being truly relevant to others. *Webster's* defines "aspiration" as "a strong desire to achieve something high or great." Most people would be pleased to hear that someone had described them as a "great person." But people don't tend to hand out that label randomly. The lesson:

> *Relevance is something we earn by the importance others place on what we do for them and by their judgment of how well we do it.*

Strong Personal Brands Are Consistent

The third component in building a strong brand is consistency— doing things that are both distinctive and relevant, and doing them again and again and again. Consistency is a hallmark of all strong brands. As a brand, you only get "credit" (acknowledgment, acceptance, or recognition by others) for what you do consistently. Consistent behaviors define your brand more clearly and concisely than the most polished and practiced patter.

- McDonald's is a fast-food icon because, regardless of the location you visit, the hamburgers, cheeseburgers, and Big Macs it serves are the same, again and again and again.
- Whether you are a regular guest at a Ritz-Carlton or a Motel 6, you go back to their properties on a regular basis because you know you can depend on them to consistently deliver what they promise.
- In the American public's consciousness—even for people who have never met them and may not like or even agree with them—figures such as Ralph Nader, Gloria Steinem, Rush Limbaugh, Maya Angelou, Ronald Reagan, and countless others stand as strong personal brands based on the consistency of their actions. In other countries and cultures, the list of names changes but the stature doesn't.

Which strongly branded public figures an individual labels admirable and which ones they label not so admirable will vary based on point of view. Everyone defines distinctiveness in their own terms. Each public figure's relevance to your needs and values will also vary. But like them or not, need them or not, you feel you know what to expect from these people because their behavior has been so consistent over so many years.

In a relationship, consistency is established by dependability of behavior. Over time, people learn that they can trust you if they experience consistent trustworthy behaviors. In the absence of personal experience, they may decide to trust you because of what they have learned of your track record from others. Your previous actions—not your intentions—lead them to believe that you can be counted on to behave in a similar way again. And every time you behave the way they expect, you reinforce the strength of your brand with them. Trust grows.

Conversely, the quickest way to diminish and ultimately destroy someone's trust is to become inconsistent. No matter how high the highs may have been, roller-coaster behavior will work against the long-term prospects of any relationship. The lesson:

> *Consistency is the hallmark of all strong personal brands.*
> *Inconsistency weakens brands and suspends belief.*

The Power of Example

Some people live decades and never really achieve a lasting impact on the people around them. Some leave a lasting legacy based on just a few short years. The latter group has brands that stand the test of time, even though time itself is denied to them in any great amount.

An excellent example is Canadian Terry Fox, who was the subject of David's award-winning film, *The Power Purpose.* At the age of eighteen, he was diagnosed with bone cancer. His right leg was amputated six inches above the knee, and he spent a long time in the hospital in recovery and rehabilitation. While there, he was moved by the suffering he saw all around him—so moved that he decided to do something about it. Three years after losing his leg, he vowed to run across Canada to raise money for cancer research. His goal: Raise at least one dollar for every man, woman, and child in the country—over twenty-four million dollars.

He started in mid-April, dipping his artificial foot in the Atlantic Ocean. During the next 143 days, initial casual interest turned into a national phenomenon. Terry Fox was running forty-two kilometers (over twenty-five miles) a day. On September 1, just east of Thunder

Bay, Ontario—two-thirds of the way to the Pacific and over fifty-three hundred kilometers from his starting point—his run came to a premature end. His cancer had returned. He died the following June, one month before his twenty-third birthday.

Terry Fox lived, however, to see what many had described as the "impossible" fundraising goal of twenty-four million dollars reached and exceeded. He raised twenty-eight million dollars.

Those who knew Terry were quick to say that he was no saint. But he showed a tremendous integrity about why he was running and what the money he raised was going for, and he would not allow anyone to muddy the waters. He made sure that all of his expenses were covered by sponsorships or contributions so every dollar donated actually went to cancer research. He made every step count.

That was in 1981. Today, Terry Fox Runs are held in more than sixty countries, from Albania to Zimbabwe. The extraordinary legacy he left—directed now by the Terry Fox Foundation in Toronto, Ontario—has raised more than a quarter of a billion dollars for cancer research. In 1999, a national survey conducted by the Dominion Institute and The Council for Canadian Unity found that in the minds of his countrymen, Terry Fox is Canada's greatest hero.

Our journeys through life may not be as dramatic as Terry Fox's, but when our values lead to distinctive, relevant, and consistent actions, the effects we have on the world around us can transcend the limits of time and place and transform the lives of others.

Climbing the Brand Ladder

Because of the dynamic nature of a relationship, the process of being distinctive, relevant, and consistent has some subtle shadings. Each interaction builds on the one before it and sets the stage for the one that will follow. As the relationship deepens and grows, it acquires a history—a breadth and depth that takes on increasing significance over time.

When you look back to your first experiences with someone important in your life, do you find yourself marveling at how little you knew about each other? From the perspective of time and experience, you can see that your relationship now exists at a much higher level. It's as though you'd been climbing a ladder, with each rung taking your relationship to a new level.

In business, the concept of **brand ladders** is used to determine how, through repeated encounters, distinctive product and service features connect with the relevant emotional needs and values of customers. The purpose is to ensure that depth and breadth is being built in the relationship. Each step leads to another, gradually getting closer to the emotional core that makes for enduring relationships.

When you open a checking account, your brand-based expectations for choosing one bank over another are likely to be pretty simple. "Keep my money safe for me until I need it. Send me a clear, accurate statement periodically. Be open enough hours and in enough locations to make it convenient for me to do business with you."

Those are lower rungs on the bank's brand ladder. But then one day you need something more—a mortgage, a loan for a new car, or a savings program for the kids' college fund. Now the bank's brand connection has a chance to move up your emotional ladder. You likely place a different—and significantly higher—value on your home or your children's future than you do on your checking account. As the bank justifies your trust at this higher level, the brand connection moves up a rung.

The same dynamic works on a personal scale as well. We start by finding out what is initially distinctive and relevant to someone else. What are their values and beliefs? What do they stand for? What do they need from others in a relationship? What, in particular, do they need from you in the beginning stages of your relationship?

The brand connection grows as you use this knowledge to progressively work your way up their ladder of ideas, desires, and values.

The experience and insight you gain as you move up the scale allows you to better understand the higher-level benefits and emotional rewards they derive from connecting with you consistently. First contacts often are tentative: neither person involved is quite sure what to expect. As our relationships move to higher levels of emotional connection, we seem to instinctively know what someone needs from us, and often don't have to think twice to provide it.

When a mother or father asks a child at dinner, "Is your food okay?" they want to make sure things taste right. That's a lower rung on the brand ladder of "parent." But an enthusiastic—especially an unsolicited—"Wow, this is really good. Thanks!" says a lot more than that the meal is okay. It says that the child values the time spent on her behalf, which makes Mom or Dad feel appreciated. That's a higher step on the ladder.

When that feeling of being appreciated is relevant to what people believe are their responsibilities, a much higher level of connection has been achieved. Their values are reinforced—which means that, in our example, finding the time to be together at mealtimes is likely to continue to be an important part of building the relationship between parent and child.

Some Reflections on Building Your Brand

Because of the back-and-forth nature of a relationship, a commitment to being distinctive and relevant to others has important carryover effects for you. Determining ways to be relevant to others reflects your desire to learn and grow. This, in turn, is expressed by continually creating, solving problems, and making things better for others and yourself.

But because someone else determines whether you're effective at brand building or not, your relevance to that person is ultimately their decision. And sometimes the connection just simply won't be there.

You won't always get along with everybody. You can't. Nobody can. Your values, however distinctive, simply won't appeal to everyone. Neither will they be relevant to everyone. You can't be all things to all people, nor should you try to be.

So one key determination you need to make in building your brand is how relevant other people are, or can be, to you. If you're going to be true to yourself and be acknowledged, accepted, and recognized for who you really are, your core values must be respected in each relationship, not compromised. To think you will never leave someone dissatisfied runs counter to the idea of a strong personal brand. So you also have to decide if any particular relationship is worth the effort.

Clarity in relationships is a key advantage of a strong personal brand. As your brand becomes better defined, people find it easier to figure out where you stand and, consequently, what value you can represent for them. They'll learn to respect your values because it will be clearer to them that those values are of utmost importance to you. As a result, they won't expect you to act in a way that contradicts those values. The payoff for you is that the number of conflicts in your life will likely diminish.

Strong vs. Moral

Brand building is not the same thing as morality in the spiritual sense—though there are, to be sure, a lot of common elements. Everyone knows people who have clearly defined brands as well as character traits and behavior patterns we (or others) may find anything from mildly distasteful to absolutely horrifying.

Think, for example, of convicted mobster John Gotti. Strong brand? Absolutely. People who knew him knew exactly what he stood for, what his values were, how he could be counted on to act in a given situation. Did that make his brand attractive? To some people (those to whom his distinctive actions and values were consistently relevant), yes. To most, no. In essence, it was strong for all the wrong reasons. But in selected relationships, he clearly established a strong personal brand.

The actions that someone else values highly may not be as relevant to you, may not be valued by you, and may even be or seem contrary to your own needs and desires. So you assign a lower, more negative value to that individual's personal brand—at least as *you* experience it. Yet sometimes everyone has to acknowledge that the individual in question is succeeding in building strong personal brand relationships with others.

Stand for Your Brand

Not all brands are attractive to us. Your values are *your* values. Our values are *ours*. We won't presume to judge them against a universal scale of right or wrong. Figuring out the "right thing" for you—that's *your* job.

When your actions and your behavior reflect your values, the result is integrity. The pieces fit. The picture you present to others is in focus, not blurred around the edges or incomplete. As stated above, we'll come back to values clarification at greater length in Chapter 4. For now, though, it is vital to appreciate that acting in concert with your values not only affects your relationships with others, it also has a highly positive effect on your relationship with yourself.

For purposes of this analysis, the "right way" to go about building a strong personal brand is to make sure your brand resonates and is relevant, in the most distinctive way possible, for those people with whom you want to build strong relationships on a long-term basis. The "wrong way" is not to develop a distinctive, relevant, consistent brand at all—to base your behaviors on inconsistent, ever-shifting values that aren't clear to you or anyone else.

As noted earlier, building a strong personal brand takes courage—because consistency takes courage. You not only need to be clear about what you believe, you need to be willing to base your actions on those beliefs time after time, no matter how great the temptation may be to compromise those beliefs. The way to make a distinctive, enduring, positive impression on someone else is to ensure that who you are, what you say you are, and what that person experiences from you are the same, time and time again.

To see that in greater detail, we're going to explore a three-dimensional model for understanding how people perceive your brand.

3 Personal Brand Dimensions

Roles, Standards, and Style

The concept of branding has been around for a long time. By one count, more than 275 books, virtually all business-oriented, have been written on this topic over the last twenty-five years. Although there are many good ideas in that material, it is often difficult to reduce the process to practical, manageable terms.

Dissatisfied with the complexity so often found in other approaches to brand building, Karl's company, Beyond Marketing Thought, has invested over a million dollars to date in market research to validate an alternative—and much simpler—model that is now helping a growing number of businesses effectively define their brands.

In this chapter, we'll adapt the business model to the realities of building a personal brand.

Changing the Focus

In Chapter 2, we showed you that from the vantage point of someone else, your brand takes shape as a result of your ability to make what you do distinctive, relevant, and consistent to that person. The Personal Brand Dimensions Model™ (to which we turn our attention now) is designed to show you what you look like to someone else—what specific attributes go into the image of your brand they carry around with them in their mind.

Personal Brand Dimensions Model

In over twenty years of working with businesses in a variety of industries and market situations, our experience suggests that people connect to a brand through three interrelated dimensions: **competencies, standards,** and **style.**

Almost always, a business brand relationship starts on the basis of a product's or service's perceived competencies—its ability to meet a need or satisfy a desire. Over time, the brand differentiates itself by moving beyond competencies through what customers perceive as a combination of standards and style. As this process evolves, the relationship builds **brand equity**—cumulative levels of credibility, trust, and value—in the customers' minds.

For personal branding, the model above combines these three distinct but interrelated dimensions in a similar fashion:

- **It identifies your brand roles:** The first brand dimension refers to the basic nature of the relationship and the things you need to do capably just to meet someone's basic expectations. It might help to think of this in terms of the role you play for another person: friend or neighbor, parent or boss, mechanic or physician—sometimes a combination of roles.

- **It establishes your brand standards:** The idea of a competent parent or friend or mechanic is somewhat generic. The second brand dimension starts to make your brand image much more specific by focusing on the way you deliver your roles. Our brand standards are the level of performance that we are willing to adhere to consistently.
- **It displays your brand style:** The third dimension in the model is the manner in which we communicate and interact with others. This is how we personalize our roles within the context of our performance standards. Think of brand style as the emotional image developed—not just through first impressions but from repeated contacts—as we interact with others.

As a relationship evolves and grows, these dimensions will evolve as well but in different ways.

- The roles at the heart of the relationship will usually remain relatively constant over time. Change here will typically be progressive and incremental in nature.
- Standards will tend to become more defined as experience clarifies expectations. Change here will involve greater precision and accuracy as we learn in greater detail what someone else needs from us.
- Style changes will reflect a growing level of familiarity, even intimacy. As each person in the relationship gains an ever better sense of what behaviors will best maintain, nurture, and deepen the connection between them, continuing adjustments here cement the bond.

You're always a parent, in other words, but the competencies needed to effectively parent a three-year-old child and a thirteen-year-old child are vastly different. In a work setting, the same principle applies to managing a twenty-six-year-old employee and a forty-six-year-old employee. The standards you'll apply to your actions also change as your child grows and develops or the relationship with your employee matures. And through the years, your style of parenting or leadership will be crystallized in the countless encounters between you and your child or you and your employee.

Working Distinctions

There are three important caveats to keep in mind as we explore the Personal Brand Dimensions Model.

First, perception is reality. The credit you receive for your brand's roles, standards, and style will be given by someone else. You will determine and decide what you want your brand dimensions to be. But that doesn't settle the issue. Only actions count. What the other person in the relationship perceives determines the success or failure of your efforts.

Second, the key perceptions that exist and persist in people's minds are the ones that are most distinctive, relevant, and consistent to *them* about *you*. In other words, what matters is how they feel about your values, how important they feel you are to their lives, and whether or not they feel they can trust you.

And third, we're using the terms "roles," "standards," and "style" in the specific context of brand building. In a business context, the Brand Dimensions Model uses the terms "competencies," "standards," and "style." Because these words are in common usage, they often have slightly different shades of meaning in other applications. "Competencies," in particular, is a much-used word in business today. Organizations focus on core competencies. Certification efforts in a variety of professional fields seek to assure demonstrated competencies. Similarly, "standards" often reflect the idea of industry norms, and "style" has fashion connotations.

The Look of a Personal Brand

To see how roles, standards, and style interrelate, consider the relationship between a parent and a child. There are billions of such relationships, each one unique, but most involve some common characteristics.

- Being a parent in the general sense suggests certain forms of competencies (abilities or skills) that come with the role: being a counselor, guide, caregiver, mentor, and so forth.
- When you tighten the focus to your own father or mother, that foundation of competencies supports a sense of specific standards (levels of performance) displayed by your particular parents. They had their own way of handling family time, setting rules, helping with homework, preparing meals, defining limits, providing discipline, planning vacations, handing out allowances, and the like. It wasn't quite the same as the way your friends' parents did things, but the different approaches still fit under the role of parent.
- Beyond those things, however, there's also a rich vein of emotional experience that comes to mind when you think of your parents' particular style of behavior. Their tone of voice, their attitudes, their facial expressions and body language—all go well beyond what they did to define a special style of doing it. Their style dimensions tend to involve highly subjective descriptions: upbeat or cynical, always in a hurry or very reflective, conservative or a little wacky, warm and loving or reserved and controlled.

Taken together, the unique combination of roles, standards, and style demonstrated to you over the years by your parents—and modified by how you reacted and interacted with them—defines a unique and memorable relationship in your life. It's a "branded" relationship. It may have much in common with the parent-child relationships your friends recall, or that you have with your own children. But it's nonetheless different, personal, and anything but a generic experience.

The way you communicate and act when you do what you do (your style) and the norms within which you consistently operate (your standards) allow you to meet some basic needs of someone else (your roles) in each meaningful relationship in your life. When your brand is clearly defined and strongly maintained, the result is an impression as distinctive and uniquely personal as a fingerprint.

Let's examine each part of the Personal Brand Dimensions Model in more detail.

Roles: Our Relationship with Others

In business, when consumers think about a brand—whether it represents a product, a service, a company, or an employer—often they first describe it based on what it does for them. Regardless of how it was built (standards) or how it looks (style), a car has to start, move, stop, keep the rain out, and keep the passengers in (roles). Regardless of how it was cooked (standards) or arranged on the plate (style), a meal has to be palatable and bear a reasonable resemblance to what the customer ordered (competencies).

Building a strong personal brand starts from a similar base. To be competent means to be, at some level, qualified (or, more accurately, *perceived* to be qualified) to do something for someone. Your roles are the fundamental reason you are in a particular relationship with another person: father or mother, sister or brother, boss, attorney, friend, financial or spiritual advisor, spouse or former spouse, nurse, mechanic, etc. An expectation on the part of the other person that you are, or can be, competent forms the basis for the relationship.

McDonald's and Wendy's both make hamburgers very competently. Although they may have successfully differentiated them-

selves in the public's minds based on standards and style, their basic competencies are very similar—preparing and serving hot food in a clean setting at a sustainable price. They have to be able to do those things just to be in the hamburger business. If they can't cook, dress, and wrap a burger, or the place is perceived as unhealthy, or the cost of doing what they do is higher than someone will pay (or the price they charge so low that it doesn't cover their cost of doing business), they won't last.

Similarly, before you can begin to make your personal brand distinctively different, you must ensure that you have demonstrated to the person with whom you want a relationship that you can competently meet their baseline needs and desires. A prospective heart surgeon who faints at the sight of blood or an apprentice electrician who can't seem to grasp the importance of not sticking metal tools into live outlets has little chance of succeeding. If you can't establish your roles, differentiation will never get to be an issue because the fundamental foundation of the relationship will never be established or will quickly fall apart.

Remember Chip Bell from Chapter 1? Here's the roles part of his Personal Brand Dimensions Model (as we would diagram it). You can see that he relates to different people in different ways: as a speaker, writer, father, husband, and so forth. Before his infectious enthusiasm

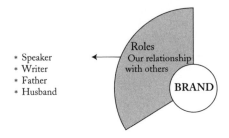

* Speaker
* Writer
* Father
* Husband

can begin to differentiate him in someone else's mind, he must be able to demonstrate his ability to competently do what needs to be done in each relationship setting.

To develop a strong personal brand, start by identifying the nature of the key relationships you plan to have. You must be insightful and realistic about the types of relationships that will support your journey to success, and clearheaded in your assessment of your own ability and willingness to offer the roles required.

Remember, however, that regardless of how you assess your roles, in the final analysis, it's the "customer"—the all-important other party in the relationship—who sets the bar for you. You can't control their perceptions, but you can and do guide people to see you as you should be seen, based on your knowledge of what they need and want from you in a relationship. The deeper the relationship, the more your mutual understanding grows.

Standards: How You Do It

If roles is the noun part of a brand, standards and style are the modifiers—the descriptive adverbs and adjectives that create a uniquely detailed picture of your brand in someone's mind. Standards are often measurable or can be defined somewhat objectively.

EXAMPLES OF PERSONAL BRAND STANDARDS

Nonjudgmental listener	Assertively opinionated
Proficient networker	Focused on a closed circle of contacts
Consistent values	Situational values
Reliably efficient	Creatively undisciplined
Open-minded/flexible	Straight/orthodox
Consensus-oriented	Independent and self-directed

As you can see, standards that can be positive and attractive to one person might be considered negative, even oV-putting, to another. That's the nature of relationships — diVerent strokes for diVerent folks. The needs of the relationship define standards that will be considered appropriate or inappropriate.

The point is not to constantly change your standards of behavior in a manic quest to try to please everybody, no matter how different their needs and expectations or how incompatible their values and yours. Focus your standards on the relationships you choose to build with people who truly matter to you.

Your standards significantly influence how others perceive you. Far beyond the basic form of roles involved in the relationship, standards begin to define and give substance to the strength of your personal brand. Consequently, even though your roles in a given area may be the same as many others, your brand standards help you stand out from the crowd.

For example, if you want people to perceive you as really committed to doing a great job, what are your quality standards? Are you prepared to make sure that every detail is covered, however long it takes, or focused on those most essential to getting the job done? The "however-long-it-takes" attention to detail that might delight one person could drive another over the edge.

Similarly, are you a take-charge person, more directive when it comes to solving problems, or do you hold back and let others try to work things out for themselves? Are you flexible in your approaches or highly systematic? Are you high-priced or budget-based? Highly tolerant or very demanding? High-maintenance or low-stress? Technologically adept or not?

In a given situation, different people will respond in different ways. It's up to the person to whom they're responding to determine the standards that are distinctive and relevant to their needs. If you're prepared to provide behavior that matches the other person's standards of distinctiveness and relevance, the relationship is worth developing. If not, you have to decide whether it's the right fit for you or whether your standards need to change to create a better fit.

Examining standards holds up a very useful—but not always flattering—mirror. For example, if you want your boss, subordinates, colleagues, or coworkers to perceive you to be on the cutting edge in a given area, how much time do you set aside for personal research and development? You might say you have competencies in a given area. But until you demonstrate those competencies in a distinctive and relevant way on a consistent basis, you can't expect to be given full credit for your claim.

Similarly, if you want to be valued for a strong personal brand at home, what is your level of investment in your relationships with your spouse and children? How much of your time, talent, and attention do you give them? If you want your friends to know they can count on

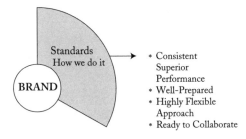

you, what evidence do they have upon which to base that judgment? How do you define being there for them? Is that the level of performance they expect and need?

To build a strong personal brand, it's critical to recognize that people cannot see your intentions. They can only see your actions. But from their perceptions of those actions, they make judgments about your standards as well as your roles—not only about what you do but how well you choose to do it.

Above is what Chip Bell's Personal Brand Dimensions Model looks like with standards added. Note that there can be some crossover between standards and style. Being professional sets a standard of performance, but it's also a recognizable style of behavior. Note also that the idea of being a nice guy still doesn't really appear. That's more specifically a style—and that comes next.

Style: How You Relate

Style is your brand's personality. It's the subjective counterpart to the more objective attributes of standards—the part that makes you uniquely yourself in someone else's mind.

Often the words people use to describe style elements will have a strong emotional tinge: friendly, easygoing, intense, aggressive, pro-

fessional, fun, energetic, introverted, extroverted, controlling, free-spirited, open, or biased. It's not uncommon, in fact, for people to describe different brands in their lives (people and their experiences with them) strictly in terms of style. We say someone is really fun. They're whimsical. They're stodgy. They're flexible. They're arrogant. They're happy. They're conservative. They're creative. Although we may regard these as descriptions of a personality, they are also essentially style components.

Note that these words tend to be subjective, not overtly measurable. Yet because a strong brand builds an emotional connection, they can carry just as much weight as more quantifiable standards. Here's where a lot of the "coloring" in a relationship comes in. Style cannot have real impact or significantly contribute to the building of a strong personal brand, however, unless the other two dimensions of roles and standards are firmly established.

On the next page is Chip Bell's completed Personal Brand Dimensions Model. Now subjective characteristics like enthusiasm and energy can take his personal brand from a basic level of roles with professional performance standards to a vibrant, uniquely memorable brand image based on an indelibly imprinted style.

The primary flaw we see in a lot of brand analysis—including some of the first attempts to adapt business brand wisdom to personal

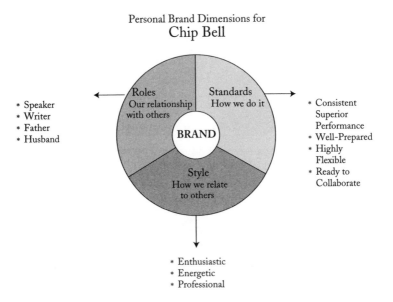

Personal Brand Dimensions for
Chip Bell

* Speaker
* Writer
* Father
* Husband

Roles
Our relationship
with others

Standards
How we do it

BRAND

Style
How we relate
to others

* Consistent
Superior
Performance
* Well-Prepared
* Highly
Flexible
* Ready to
Collaborate

* Enthusiastic
* Energetic
* Professional

applications—is its one-dimensional nature. Too often, the analysis ignores the substantive issues of roles and standards, shifting almost immediately to "reinventing" a superficial style designed more to provide an outward show than to express essential values.

Style is important. But image, to once again refute the common assertion, definitely is not everything. It's the proverbial tip of the iceberg—the smallest part of something but the only part that's visible. Because it shows, it's an important navigational aid. But it's still only a small part of something much larger and deeper.

Building a Brand Picture

When we assemble the Personal Brand Dimensions Model of an individual like Chip Bell, you can start to see how the pieces interlock and strengthen each other. Roles are the foundation upon which you begin to build your brand. Taken alone, however, your roles may be quite similar to those of many others. Roles are a starting point, but they don't provide differentiation. That comes from standards and style.

Obviously, multiple brands can coexist. For example, we've established that Wendy's and McDonald's are both competent at making hamburgers. The loyalty of their particular customers is gained through their very different approaches to the issues of standards and style. McDonald's customers, who tend to be family-oriented, want food their children recognize and won't turn up their noses at. They also want it at a price that's friendly to the family budget. Wendy's customers want a juicier burger, are willing to wait while it's assembled, and don't mind paying a slightly higher price for it. Same basic competencies. Different standards and style.

Making It Personal

Together, your combination of roles, standards, and style builds a distinctive, relevant, and consistent brand image in someone else's mind. From that brand image, people know what to expect from you and can make informed decisions about the role they want you to play in their lives.

It's important—and, we hope, somewhat comforting—to understand that to be a strong brand doesn't mean you have to appeal to everyone. Just as businesses do, you can target your brand to specific relationships.

The typical McDonald's is built for scale—a large service counter and volume-oriented systems. It sells many times more items than Wendy's does. But because Wendy's builds on its burger competencies with different standards and style, its restaurants have smaller counters and less volume yet still succeed—both in the eyes of customers and by the bottom-line standards of today's business world.

Applebee's and Chili's serve up even fewer burgers but can be judged every bit as satisfying according to the standards and style preferences of their own loyal customers.

Usually, authors offer celebrities as brand models: high-profile actors and actresses, entrepreneurs and artists, famous people drawn from history or the day's headlines. It's unlikely you've ever heard of or will ever encounter James Scothorn. It's perhaps slightly more likely you'll be affected by Dr. David Dunn. But we believe their absence of notoriety makes them even better exemplars of how to assemble a coherent, desirable combination of roles, standards, and style.

James Scothorn

James Scothorn is a straightforward, free-spirited, compassionate, and gentle person. When we use the Personal Brand Dimensions Model to illustrate his strengths, the roles list includes "marketing communications specialist" and "father"; standards and style involve attributes such as "professional," "open-minded," "compassionate," "attentive to detail," and "fun."

As it turns out, James was once a hippie. But while he has adjusted his style to the more conventional world in which he now lives, he's never lost the free-spirited, compassionate value system that was an essential part of his former lifestyle. He has been able to translate the engaging attitudes of his former life into enduring relationships that permeate his current life.

He has built a successful career as a marketing communications professional. He has served successful stints as a cardiopulmonary therapist, grade-school teacher, university instructor, and musician. In every case, he has focused a personally intense, grounded belief system on developing successful, enduring relationships that neither compromise his values nor mislead the people with whom he relates professionally.

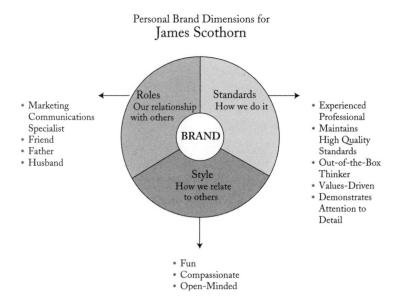

Personal Brand Dimensions for
James Scothorn

Roles
Our relationship with others

Standards
How we do it

BRAND

Style
How we relate to others

* Marketing Communications Specialist
* Friend
* Father
* Husband

* Experienced Professional
* Maintains High Quality Standards
* Out-of-the-Box Thinker
* Values-Driven
* Demonstrates Attention to Detail

* Fun
* Compassionate
* Open-Minded

James Scothorn's personal brand doesn't stop when he leaves his job, either. On more than one occasion, he has been heard to say, "My first role in life is to be a father and husband, and second to be a respected professional." James is fond of rushing home from work to get his bicycle with the double-seated trailer to pick up his twins from day care. If the leisurely ride home happens to pass along a Pacific beach, they frequently make a stop so the trio can play games in the sand.

His compassionate, gentle nature is very evident when he talks about his kids. It's equally visible in his commitment to a job in a Silicon Valley biotech firm whose work he believes offers tremendous promise for all humankind. Thus, his personal brand is anchored not only in professional marketing roles but also in standards and styles that connect to deeply held personal values.

The success he has achieved in his professional life is clearly energized by the alignment of his personal values with the values of the company he works for. His role as husband and father is energized by the belief system he has adhered to inwardly for decades. In all respects, James has been able to link his belief system with all parts of his life, allowing him to be more of who he is, not less.

Dr. David Dunn

In their element—an operating room—you expect surgeons to be organized, meticulous, and obsessed with details. Dr. Dunn, who heads the Department of Surgery at the University of Minnesota, an internationally renowned hospital, doesn't disappoint in that regard. His brand begins with his role as a transplant surgeon.

However, what really begins to drive home the strength of his brand are the standards he sets—and lives by—not only inside the operating room, but outside as well. Wherever he is, a level of conscientiousness bordering on perfectionism characterizes everything he does, from surgeries that can last more than eight hours at a time to an hour spent as a committee representative on a task force.

For Karl, Dr. Dunn's distinctive approach to standards and style became personally relevant (and highly memorable) one morning in a boardroom setting. Instead of slides or overheads, Karl likes to use storyboards (slides mounted on chipboard, about 18" x 24") for visual reinforcement. The room that day was cramped enough that he made his presentation sitting down, without the benefit of the usual easel to hold the storyboards.

As it happened, David Dunn was in the next chair. Karl, who was aware of his impressive medical reputation, made the simple decision, based on convenience, to ask him to hold the boards as Karl finished with them. Without a hint of self-consciousness about position or power, Dr. Dunn readily agreed. The presentation proceeded uneventfully. The task force covered what needed to be covered. The session finished up.

When it was over, this immensely respected physician handed back the boards—and another piece of anecdotal evidence of what it looks

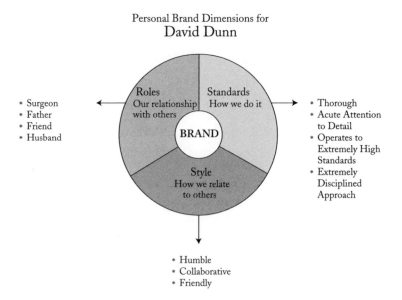

Personal Brand Dimensions for
David Dunn

* Surgeon
* Father
* Friend
* Husband

Roles
Our relationship with others

Standards
How we do it

BRAND

Style
How we relate to others

* Thorough
* Acute Attention to Detail
* Operates to Extremely High Standards
* Extremely Disciplined Approach

* Humble
* Collaborative
* Friendly

like when people truly live their brands. As he handed back the boards, he said, "Remember, now, they're in reverse order."

The man brings that kind of attention to detail to even the most simple nonwork situations. You'd expect that kind of concentrated focus from a nationally renowned surgeon. But even when he's handling someone else's presentation slides instead of his own instruments?

Obviously, that kind of thoroughness—that unassuming approach to "living a brand" every waking minute—made a lasting impression. His personal brand standards and style of thoroughness, attention to detail, perfectionism, humility, and cooperation clearly showed through.

Different Is Imperative

James Scothorn and David Dunn are very different people in very different occupations and family settings. Yet each has developed a strong personal brand that resonates with the needs of the people in their lives. That illustrates a key point about personal brands: Because different people want and need different things, very different brands can thrive and prosper side by side. There are no absolutes where brands are involved. Brands (personal as well as business) truly are interactive relationships, not static statements.

In either world, a brand is not a product of advertising. It's not packaging. It's not outward appearances. A great brand has equity because people can cut right through the external trappings and see the value in associating with it. If you compromise on roles, standards, and style, you can't become a strong personal brand, any more than McDonald's can compromise on food quality, or Ritz-Carlton can rent out rooms that haven't been cleaned, or FedEx can deliver next week instead of tomorrow.

The effective combination of competencies, standards, and style makes a great business brand. The same combination will make you a great personal brand as well. And when you can anchor the relationships in your life to values deeply rooted in your soul, you take the idea of brand to a whole new level. That's where we'll take you next.

4 | Personal Brand Authenticity

Purpose, Vision, and Values

So far, we've focused primarily on the external side of what it takes to build a strong personal brand—the elements and attributes that strengthen relationships, as perceived and judged by the other person involved in those relationships. We've relied on examples and observations to give you a general understanding of how brands work. Now we're going to turn inside and look at what drives and inspires those people who build strong personal brands.

Values with Value

Our approach to personal branding is based on the premise that values are important. Brands have values. People have values. Most people would say they desire to live according to their values. But in our high-speed, hectic world, many people have come to feel that their values are in conflict with those of the world around them. Many, in fact, feel they are being asked—even forced—to compromise their personal values to get along with others or to be successful. "Winning is the only thing" is a common philosophy. The personal costs can be added up later.

We don't believe that. To the contrary, we believe that people can be enormously successful *because of*, rather than in spite of, their values. When your values align with the values of your peers, your family, your customers, and your organizations, life becomes a much more harmonious experience.

And that harmony can only be achieved by holding on to who you are. It's achieved by being committed to and holding on to your essential values. Call it integrity, authenticity, being true to yourself, or any number of other things. No matter how it is named, the results are greater peace of mind, a more rewarding life, and an enhanced sense of your own self-worth.

We maintain that a successful brand is an accurate, genuine representation of the substance at the core of the originator, be it a business or an individual. To get credit (acknowledgment, acceptance, recognition) for that reality, the originator has to actively live their brand's values every day, testing them in the "marketplace" of personal and professional relationships and watching how others accept or reject those values. Ultimately, whether or not a personal brand is strong and viable will be revealed in the depth and breadth of the relationships that do or do not take form.

It all starts with, and continuously loops back to, the way you integrate your values into your life. And as we've emphasized, the objective is not just to use your values as the bedrock for a strong personal brand but also to get credit, to be positively acknowledged for those values from the world around you. Without credit for your values, in terms of your brand, your commitment to those values cannot be fully realized. The world—as evidenced through your relationships—isn't seeing that vital connection. It isn't seeing the "real you."

In helping you build and maintain a personal brand as a means to success, we cannot stress this idea of relationships—of connection—enough. We have nothing against (in fact, we encourage) taking time alone, reading uplifting books, watching motivational videos, or anything else that promotes personal development. But in the end, to succeed, you need to make a meaningful connection with somebody else.

It's a familiar pattern:

- A scientist will work alone for weeks, months, even years, gaining new knowledge and making exciting discoveries inside the lab. But until the results are tested and validated in the "real world," all that time and effort doesn't begin to pay off.

- The difference between a garage band and an international phenomenon, Shakespearean soliloquies recited in the shower or from center stage, is the presence or absence of a connection with a larger world.

- The great American poet Emily Dickinson worked for years in an upstairs room, the fruits of her genius carefully wrapped in ribboned packets and stowed in a trunk. Only after her death, when her sister discovered her work and sought to have it published, did her writing begin to have an effect on the world.

Whether you seek to achieve career goals, financial goals, family goals, altruistic goals, or any combination thereof, a strong personal brand will succeed for you only to the extent that you put it actively and purposefully to work in the world around you.

Authenticity: Time to Step Up

The most intimate relationship you have is with yourself. Consequently, a strong personal brand is a powerful way for the world to see and value the authentic you. Therefore, the process of brand building involves a certain amount of introspection.

The dictionary defines "authentic" as "true to one's own personality, spirit, or character." When it comes to relationships, authenticity is what others say they want most from us. We make the most lasting and vivid impressions when people witness us being true to our beliefs, staying in alignment with who and what we really are. That's authenticity.

When you summon the courage to be authentic, the effect is powerful. Trust is built faster and maintained longer when people believe you are being real, not putting on a false front to cover up what's really going on inside of you. Authenticity doesn't come easily, however. For, as we have intimated previously, courage is not in abundant supply in our world.

If you stop here for a moment, you might hear something inside you at this point that sounds like this: "An inspiring notion, but you guys are just too idealistic. Very noble, but the world just doesn't operate that way. I would love to be genuine and authentic, but where I work the culture wouldn't support it." It doesn't take long at all for the little but-but-buts to start sounding like a small engine, an engine on a vehicle going nowhere.

We have evidence that the world *can* work this way. Your friends and family *can* get it. Your boss and any other person with whom you have a relationship *can* and *will* develop respect for you. You can and deserve to feel better about what you're looking at in the mirror every morning. But you need to make a commitment—here and now—to work deliberately to make sure people experience you as a truly authentic person.

Close investigation of people with strong brands typically will show they have used authenticity to fuel their success. You can, too. Three very visible "signposts" can guide you on the road to authenticity:

- The first signpost is what you see as your purpose for being in this world. Why do you exist? Why are you here?
- The second signpost describes your vision. What do you want for your life? What are your dreams? What do you want to create?
- The third signpost clarifies your values. What do you hold to be true? What's important to you? What are you willing—and not willing—to do to succeed?

When someone's life is purposeless, when they exist with no vision for the future, there is no grounding for their values, no motivation to act, and nothing that inspires the desire to enrich their own lives and the lives of those who surround them. Any effort to be authentic in these circumstances, therefore, is a meaningless endeavor.

On the other hand, if you believe there is a purpose to your life, that what you envision yourself contributing to the world is important, that your values have depth and substance and merit, then it's much easier to feel inspired to discover ways to become more effective. When your purpose, vision, and values are expressed as a brand people find distinctive, relevant, and consistent, you've got something the world shows no signs of ever getting enough of.

Let's examine purpose, vision, and values in a little more detail. Then, in Chapter 6 that follows, we'll show you how to express them in a statement—a **brand promise**—that can give direction to your brand-building efforts.

First Signpost: Purpose—What Is My Life About?

Purpose is what gives meaning to everyone's lives. You can be as metaphysical or religious with this concept as you want to be, but everyone wants to believe that they matter, that there is a reason for their existence. However they reach that realization, the depth of their conviction as to why they are in the world directs the way they think and the way they behave. This, in turn, has great bearing on how they wish and choose to relate to others.

In terms of the practical realities of brand building, the more clarity you have about why you do what you do—your purpose—the greater the chance of achieving your objectives. This clarity doesn't happen automatically, however. As we've pointed out more than once, someone else has a stake in the relationship—and consequently a vital role in determining its ultimate success or failure.

To see the validity of this distinction, consider how these ideas and ideals are applied to the ever more competitive world of business. In the sales arena, for example, it appears to be a "no-brainer" that positive relationships are fundamental to success. For many years, however, sales training has largely consisted of teaching manipulative techniques that, in the name of building relationships, often damage or destroy them.

Even today, if you ask top sales executives, "What is the purpose of a salesperson?" the most common answer you'll hear is, "To close the deal." Yet customers loathe being "closed." In fact, the focus on closing is the primary reason salespeople have developed such a poor reputation.

Ironically, although people resist "being closed," they love to buy. However, they want to buy from someone they trust. In enlightened organizations, sales training has shifted its primary focus from how to close to how to successfully open and build trusting relationships.

And what is the most effective way for salespeople to build trust? To have, first and foremost, a primary purpose—solving the customers' problems and meeting their needs. When customers believe that a salesperson has their best interests at heart, they will give that person the opportunity to "earn" their business—not just once, but again and again.

In the short term, powerful persuasive abilities may allow you to settle issues with colleagues, a spouse, or a child on your own terms very quickly. But a consistent lack of interest or desire to meet their long-term needs closes down the vital lines of communication that nourish those relationships. As the effects compound, your relevance deteriorates. The result is a *weak* personal brand.

How people behave toward others, therefore, is driven by what they see as the purpose of their relationships. If they are concerned only with their own agenda, those intentions will get through and be felt by the other person no matter how "smooth" the initiating person may be. It won't take long for the other people to look elsewhere for a person willing to put their needs first.

On the other hand, when people demonstrate a consistent interest in sustaining something that may go on for a long time (perhaps a lifetime), others will experience their purpose as being genuinely concerned with their needs and desires. Their relevance to the other people's lives skyrockets. And as they express this purpose consistently over time, their personal brand grows stronger and stronger.

Second Signpost: Vision—What Do I Want to Create?

There is something magical about an unfettered, unencumbered, uninhibited child's approach to the world. David finds his five-year-old grandson, Evan, a constant source of fascination—and personal brand insights. Not distracted by the responsibilities of parenthood, David has had the luxury of observing Evan's accelerating learning curve and the unbridled joy that accompanies each new discovery.

Evan is no exception to the rules of child development. Like many children between the ages of one and five, he experiences a considerable amount of joy and happiness in day-to-day life without the stresses of the adult world intruding. Being lovingly cared for is a major reason for that joy, of course. That's the external support a child needs. But something of equal significance is going on in the lives of young children: they are constantly involved in the act of *creation*.

To create means to bring into being something that has never existed before. For children, virtually everything is a new discovery—about themselves, about the important people in their world, about that world in general. Their unrelenting curiosity ignites the phenomenal growth they experience intellectually and emotionally. They are immersed in that wonderful time where the "big people" haven't yet started telling them what they won't be able to do. Their vision has no limits at this age. Anything and everything is possible.

Of course, eventually the fairy tale is exposed. The unlimited vision of life's possibilities becomes progressively more limited. Some of this is simply a necessary process of developing a practical appreciation for reality—children learning they can't fly like Superman, or sing like Streisand, or make all of the people and forces around them behave in precisely the ways they want them to.

But some of it also is a result of learning to perceive limits where none exist, of making unconscious decisions that harden over time into barriers the growing child considers more powerful than they may actually be. Those barriers may keep him or her from acting when the only thing that's holding them together is a perception in their minds.

In his numerous books (including *Repacking Your Bags* [Berrett-Koehler, 1996] and, most recently, *Whistle While You Work* [Berrett-Koehler, 2001]), career and life planning expert Dick Leider provides valuable insights into the consequences of lost visions. When someone tells him they feel hemmed in by the circumstances of their life, he's prone to ask, "Suppose that an eighteen year old walked up to you at this moment and said, 'Here's exactly what you're going to do with the next twenty to forty years of your life.' How would you react?"

Odds are most people would, at best, find such unsolicited advice laughable. At worst, they'd be outraged. After all, what possibly qualifies an eighteen year old, a mere teenager, to lay out a meaningful course for their lives?

That is precisely Leider's point. For many people, the essential decisions that directed the course they have been on for twenty years or more were based on decisions made when they were about eighteen years old. Unfortunately, from the limited perspective available at that age, those decisions rarely took into account such life-enhancing questions as, What do I believe in? What do I want to contribute? What do I want to create for my life? Rather, the needs of the moment may have focused on more tangible issues, such as pay and security or getting through whatever seemed to be the most immediate crisis they faced. Not the stuff to stir the soul, is it?

Small wonder that the personal brand many people unconsciously develop doesn't cast a very distinct shadow. It has been years—decades, in some cases—since they gave any real thought to what the world they want to be living in *should* look like, instead of what it does look like.

We believe rediscovering what lights you up internally is an important part of the personal brand-building process, a means to reconnect what's most authentically you with the important people in the world around you. It reignites your passions and makes you come alive. When Braveheart's William Wallace (as portrayed by Mel Gibson) observes that "Many people are born, but few people truly live," he is trying to convince his people not to settle for mere existence, but to envision, work for, and ultimately fight for, the freedom to choose a future that reflects the way they want to live and the lives they truly want to lead.

Whether you have a clear vision of the future you're trying to create for yourself and the important others in your life, or it has been years since you've updated the childlike sense of possibilities that once was so powerful a part of you, your life is meant to be a process of purposeful creation. And it can't be stopped by forces outside of you. It begins again at your discretion, whenever you choose.

Therefore, wherever you are, and however far that is from where you want to be, you can combine the knowledge and wisdom you've gained through the long, hard years with the sense of possibilities you once had, to define a vision that truly represents what you want for your life.

Life is never more rich, more full, or more rewarding than when you are moving faithfully and persistently toward a compelling vision. When you are purposefully creating, you become fully alive. That vitality imbues your personal brand with an essential energy that can make it even more viable and attractive.

Third Signpost: Values—What Do I Hold to Be True?

All strong brands, whether business or personal, have at their foundation a clear belief system. Yes, they may have wonderful logos, ads, and package designs, but make no mistake, it's the value provided—which reflects the values within—that people care about and are attracted to. Long term, you don't choose FedEx because of its snappy commercial slogans or UPS because its trucks are painted brown. You choose them because the reliability of their performance is a continuing demonstration of their commitment to what they believe—their values.

In business, organizations with the strongest *external* brands have the strongest *internal* values. When an organization's values are clear, they are shared by those within the organization. The result of that clarity and unanimity is that customers respond and relate to those values on a positive, emotional level.

Similarly, the values you relate to in a spouse, child, close friend, or respected mentor are beyond considerations of how they look, the position they hold, or the car they drive. You connect to something inside them. To develop a strong personal brand takes very clear values—and the commitment to build enduring relationships that reflect those values.

Brand Values Profile

In the game of life, people are constantly confronted with situations where they might feel pressured or tempted to act in ways that are contrary to their values. Those compromises are judgment calls that often confront people in unexpected ways. But they're easier to make in accordance with your values if you've given some thought to those values and how they apply to the building of your personal brand.

An important part of building a personal brand is identifying your values—what you believe and don't believe, what you hold to be true, what's important, what you respect and don't respect, and what you are willing and not willing to do to achieve your goals.

Research conducted by the Minnesota-based Meiss Education Institute finds a strong connection between understanding our most important values and making better decisions—the kind of decisions that help us develop more effective relationships with others. The Institute defines personal values as the inner rules or principles we use to make choices and run our lives. To help people identify their most closely held values, it has developed a Personal Values Profile, a portion of which we've adapted here into a Personal Brand Values Profile to help you clarify what you feel and believe strongly—your values.

This survey-style profile is not a test. You cannot pass or fail. There is no one "best" profile. Rather, this is a nonpsychometric measure of personal preferences regarding values. It is designed to help you understand yourself, recognize the issues involved in a situation at hand, and then choose values-based strategies appropriate to the situation.

Through this Personal Brand Values Profile, we'll help you to

- Identify your top seven personal values.
- Differentiate between your real values (the ones that you actually operate from) and your idealized values (the ones you think you should operate from).
- Anticipate and minimize potential conflicts with others.
- Learn to make better decisions in your work life and personal life based on your values preferences.

Step One: Read each value and place a check mark in the appropriate column to indicate its relative importance to you (not important, somewhat important, or very important). Rate all values on the list. Use the "Other" spaces to add values important to you but not included on this list.

Value Description	Not important	Somewhat important	Very important
Achievement (results, tasks completed)			X
Adventure (new experiences, challenge, excitement)			X
Artistic Expression (drama, painting, literature)		X	
Balance (proper attention to each area of life)			X
Competition (desire to win, to take risks)			X
Contribution (desire to make a difference, to give)			X
Control (desire to be in charge, sense of order)		X	
Cooperation (teamwork, working with others)		X	
Creativity (new ideas, innovation, experimenting)		X	
Economic Security (freedom from financial worries)			X
Fairness (equal chance, equal hearing for all)		X	
Fame (desire to be well-known, recognized)		X	
Family Happiness (desire to get along, respect, harmony)			X
Friendship (intimacy, caring, support)			X
Generosity (desire to give time or money readily)			X
Health (physical fitness, energy, no disease)			X
Independence (self-reliance, freedom from controls)			X
Influence (desire to shape ideas, people, processes)			X
Inner Harmony (desire to be at peace with oneself)			X
Integrity (honesty, sincerity, consistent demonstration of your values)			X
Learning (growth, knowledge, understanding)			X
Loyalty (duty, allegiance, respect)			X
Nature (care for and appreciation of the environment)		X	
Order (organization, conformity, stability)		X	
Personal Development (improvement, reach potential)			X
Pleasure (enjoyment, fun, happiness)			X
Power (authority, influence over people and/or situations)			X
Prestige (visible success, rank, status)			X
Quality (excellence, high standards, minimal errors)		X	
Recognition (respect, acknowledgment, applause)			X
Responsibility (desire to be accountable, trustworthy, mature)			X
Security (desire to feel safe about things, surroundings)			X
Service (desire to assist others, to improve society)			X

(continued)

Value Description	Not important	Somewhat important	Very important
Self Respect (pride in self, feeling worthy)			X
Spirituality (belief or interest in a higher power or God)		X	
Stability (continuity, predictability)			X
Tolerance (openness to others, their views and values)			X
Tradition (treasuring the past, customs)			X
Variety (diversity of activities and experiences)			
Wealth (material prosperity, affluence, abundance)			X
Wisdom (desire to understand life, to exercise sound judgment)			X
Other:			
Other:			
Other:			

Step Two: After checking the relative importance of all the values, look at those you checked as being "very important." Your goal for this survey is to refine your list of very important values to the seven you consider most important. Go back through the list and choose the seven values that are most important to you. Record these seven values in any order on the lines below.

Top 7 "Very Important" Values

1. _____

2. _____

3. _____

4. _____

5. _____

6. _____

7. _____

As you review your choices, give thought to whether these are values you actually have and live by or whether they are values you feel you ought to have. You may have chosen a value through a sense of loyalty to an outside influence—family, religion, employer, community, etc. That value, while not to be discounted, may not actually be among the seven values that most commonly and realistically characterize your actions. It is crucial to be honest and realistic, rather than idealistic, in your assessments. Since this is not a test, no one is going to try to impose their sense of "proper" values on you. Give your list one more review and make any changes necessary.

Congratulations! You are now in a rare group of people who actually know what is, at the core of their being, important to them. You also have just identified seven key values that will provide the starting point for what we will do next—your **brand strategy**.

5 Personal Brand Framework

Defining Your Unique Brand

In the last three chapters, we've shown you what a personal brand is and how, based on its connection to your values and beliefs, it develops in the important relationships in your life. We've discussed the underlying need to be *distinctive, relevant,* and *consistent* in your approach to the relationships that develop around your brand. We've introduced the Personal Brand Dimensions Model, which shows you how *roles, standards,* and *style* fit together into a coherent whole. We've given you a way to align these external elements with your sense of *purpose, vision,* and *values.* Now it is time to put this knowledge to work designing and building a framework through which you can manage your personal brand.

In this continuing process, you will face many of the same challenges that businesses do. Just as they do in the corporate arena, the heady pace and sheer dimensions of change in our world affect your personal life, your career, and the way you relate to people—socially, in the neighborhood, as a customer, and as a citizen. Just as they do in business, powerful forces cause the people you know and have reason to care about to place a high value on solid, strong, and trustworthy relationships.

Against this backdrop, many of the same tactics businesses rely on in building successful brands can work for you as well.

Personal Brand Management Framework

The framework we recommend for developing and managing your personal brand has three essential pieces. The first one focuses on developing a personal brand strategy. The other two provide a set of guidelines for building, measuring, and accruing personal brand equity over time.

- **Personal Brand Manifesto:** The touchstone in building a personal brand is your personal brand manifesto. Each personal brand manifesto contains three key elements—a set of personal brand dimensions, a personal brand platform, and a personal brand promise. Examples can be found in Appendix II.
  - **Personal Brand Dimensions:** the combination of roles, standards, and style that defines the unique aspects of your personal brand. In this chapter, we're going to show you how to use the model we gave you in Chapter 3 to identify and chart the key components of your brand.
  - **Personal Brand Platform:** the single dominant characteristic of your personal brand dimensions.
  - **Personal Brand Promise:** a concise, meaningful, and inspiring statement, developed from your brand dimensions and driven by your brand platform, that sums up the impact a relationship with you will have on someone else. This will be the focus of our work in Chapter 6.
- **Personal Brand Measurement:** To more closely align your tactics with your personal brand dimensions and promise, you will need ways to gauge how effectively (or ineffectively) you are meeting your objectives. We'll show you how to develop this kind of feedback in Chapter 7.
- **Personal Brand Building:** As feedback helps you refine and better manage your personal brand, you'll find there are many distinctive, relevant, and consistent ways to powerfully impact relationships. We'll also cover this subject in Chapter 7.

Making an Emotional Connection

When it comes to building a personal brand, your goal is the same as that of a business—positioning and managing your brand for long-term health and profitability. You want to create and reinforce a particular impression in the mind of someone to whom you are (or wish to become) important. To do that, you need to know who you are—what your values are—and what makes you valuable to someone else, then manage the connection between the two for maximum value.

This is a two-way street. Not only does a strong personal brand provide benefits for you, a branded relationship also provides the other person with a verifiable emotional payoff. They feel better for having interacted with you. They feel more cared for, more affirmed, more knowledgeable, more in the loop, more capable, and more empowered, just for having interacted with you.

Emotional connections are essential to strong brands, whatever their context. And the kinds of emotions that build those connections can be boiled down to a relatively finite and manageable set of variables.

In a recent study at the Stanford University Graduate School of Business, Jennifer Aaker, an assistant professor of marketing in UCLA's Anderson School of Management, reported on the results of a quest to determine the "dimensions of brand personality."

Using what behavioral scientists know about human personality variables as a starting point, researchers probed the way people use personality traits to describe brands with which they are familiar. Initially, they came up with more than three hundred unique descriptors. But when they analyzed the data, they found they could boil down the list to just forty-two traits, which in turn reflected just five distinct factors:

- Sincerity
- Excitement
- Competence
- Sophistication
- Ruggedness

For a business, brand building typically involves using a combination of these attributes to show customers what its products or services can do. Think about the way the automobile industry tries to position its products in the public's mind. They don't chatter on and on about tangible attributes—how many pounds of steel and composites go into the car, the clarity of the glass in the windshield, or the fibers used to make the carpeting on the floor. Instead, they create emotion-laden images that emphasize how the basic quality of their offerings will *feel* to people when they're behind the wheel.

What emotional payoffs do people derive from their relationships with you? Chances are, a lot of them connect to the five traits on Aaker's list. Do you help people feel there's some honest value in connecting with you (sincerity)? Do you rev them up and get them motivated (excitement)? Do you make them better able to do what they need or want to do (competence)? Do you raise the level of their knowledge and understanding, their appreciation or enjoyment (sophistication)? Do you help them deal more capably or resiliently with what life throws at them on a day-to-day basis (ruggedness)?

When you honestly assess the primary emotional payoff another person gets from being in a relationship with you, you can target your brand-building actions for maximum effect. This is not manipulative: it is knowing and understanding your brand strengths and capitalizing on them.

Your Brand Dimensions

Defining your personal brand dimensions and refining them into a personal brand platform involves identifying the roles, standards, and style that go into each relationship people have with you. For illustration, we'll build one from scratch using Jeannie Seeley-Smith as our example. (Her completed brand dimensions are on page 66.)

David serves on the board of Perspectives, a Minneapolis-based social service agency of which Seeley-Smith is the executive director. The nonprofit agency deals with the many difficult issues involved in rehabilitating the lives of families of women who have been incarcerated for minor crimes or gone through treatment for drug use and other behavioral problems. Seeing what she sees on a daily basis, Seeley-Smith could easily have become hardened or cynical. Instead, she serves as a constant champion of and example for her clients, combining personal compassion and professional savvy to help find workable solutions for people who have felt they've had too few options for far too long.

Step One: Identify the Areas Where Your Roles Matter

Your personal brand dimensions start with what you do, and need to do well, in the context of a relationship. Seeley-Smith needs to demonstrate competencies as the director of Perspectives, as a spouse, as a mother, and as a friend. These are the relationships in which her personal brand will be tested. Write down the important relationships in your life where your roles are on the line.

_____

_____

_____

_____

_____

Step Two: Examine Your Standards and Values

Remember, your personal brand strategy connects inside. The soul of your personal brand comes from your sense of purpose, vision, and values. In the context of brand dimensions, your values—not just your top seven but the whole list—very likely will help you identify standards that begin to differentiate you in your relationships.

Standards also have a performance aspect. Take a moment to reflect upon a situation when you felt you were at the top of your game. What was it about the way you approached that challenge or problem, or met that need, that revealed an outstanding part of your character? Odds are those are brand standards, too. Was it your responsiveness? Your tenacity? Your clear thinking? Your high energy? The thoughtfulness of your approach? The innovativeness of your thinking? Your unique frame of reference or set of experiences? Your specialized knowledge or expertise? Your willingness to take the lead—or be a team player or supportive resource? The three to five characteristics that consistently come to the fore when you review situations in which you performed well are brand standards.

Jeannie Seeley-Smith's standards include her absolute dedication to the women and families she works with, her political savvy in opening doors and building coalitions that can help her clients, her thoroughness, her pragmatism, the enthusiasm she brings to her work, the street smarts she has acquired (and applies) in gaining buy-in from people who aren't prone to trust quickly or easily, and her multidimensional approach to life—she's always willing to consider new information and evaluate new answers to see if they contribute to her passion.

Write down the primary standards and key values that energize your relationships.

_____

_____

_____

_____

_____

_____

_____

_____

Step Three: Define Your Style

Now think of the unique parts of your personality that make an impact on other people when you are at the top of your game. Do people consistently react to your positive attitude? Your humorous demeanor? Your straightforward approach? Your willingness to see the silver lining in every cloud? Your sense of calm? The friendliness of your approach? Your sincerity? Your inquisitiveness? Your sense of whimsy—or your formal, no-nonsense personality?

Jeannie Seeley-Smith's style is characterized by enthusiasm, realism, high energy, a positive outlook and, in particular, compassion. She's not just going through the motions with people—not at Perspectives and not at home, either. If she didn't invest as much of herself in relationships as she does, she wouldn't get the kind of results she regularly achieves, especially with people whom society in general might be more than willing to discard. She cares. She channels that caring into realistic, practical actions that reflect a desired outcome. That's what makes her so good at what she does—and such a strong brand in the lives of the people she touches.

Write down the three to five characteristics that reflect your brand style.

_____

_____

_____

_____

_____

_____

In completed form, Seeley-Smith's Personal Brand Dimensions Model looks like the figure on the next page.

Your own model may be less clear at this stage because you're just beginning to gain some familiarity with the model and where to plug

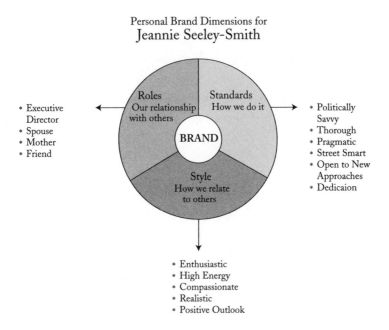

Personal Brand Dimensions for
Jeannie Seeley-Smith

* Executive
  Director
* Spouse
* Mother
* Friend

Roles
Our relationship
with others

Standards
How we do it

BRAND

Style
How we relate
to others

* Politically
  Savvy
* Thorough
* Pragmatic
* Street Smart
* Open to New
  Approaches
* Dedicaion

* Enthusiastic
* High Energy
* Compassionate
* Realistic
* Positive Outlook

in different variables. Here are some considerations that may help you clarify your personal brand dimensions:

- Compare your lists of brand standards and brand style characteristics to your list of personal values. Is there a connection? Are your brand standards and brand style characteristics supported by your proclaimed personal values? For example, if one of your brand standards is the knowledgeable way you approach problems, is it supported by a personal value of learning? If one of your brand styles is your friendly approach, did you identify friendship as a personal value? If having fun is high on your style list, is pleasure on your values list?

- What do the consistencies and inconsistencies tell you? For each brand standard and brand style, ask yourself, What is it about my approach—the way my values connect to my attitudes and my actions—that makes it more difficult to *consistently* demonstrate the standard and style characteristics I consider (or want to consider) essential to my personal brand?

- Use passion as a yardstick to gauge your priorities. Carefully examine each brand standard and style you've identified from the standpoint of your passions. The energy, enthusiasm, and visible personal commitment we bring to what we do help build the distinctive picture of our brand in people's minds. Do you demonstrate so much passion for the characteristics you've identified as important internally that all the people you relate to externally perceive them as distinctive?

- The final test is *relevancy*. As you look at the brand standards and brand style that you're employing consistently and distinctively, assess how well or how poorly they connect with what people seem to need from you. Do the brand standards and brand style characteristics that you've identified connect to the standards and style people actually want and expect from you?

Remember that although your brand's *roles* will vary depending on the nature of the relationship involved—you do, and you are valued for, different things as a parent than as an employer or an employee—your personal brand's standards and style should remain relatively constant (even distinctively so). That kind of constancy is a hallmark of a strong brand. If you're cheerful at work, you should be cheerful at home. If you have the mettle to hold up under pressure as a parent, you should be a good bet to exhibit the same resilience in the workplace.

To build strong brands over the long term, businesses make sure they're applying key brand standards and brand style characteristics in ways that are consistently and distinctively relevant to the competencies involved in each specific brand relationship. You can do the same. Over time, it becomes almost instinctive.

The Soul of a Brand

The genius of McDonald's is creating a recognizable set of distinctive, relevant, and consistent competencies, and building a business on it for a target market—families with children. When you take your children to a fancy restaurant, you will not infrequently find that they somehow think they're in a Grimm's fairy tale and you're trying to poison them. They don't care how many awards the cuisine has won. You can hear their refrain as you read this: "Have we ever had this before?" Under the Golden Arches—or in any of the host of familiar places built along similar lines—that question almost never comes up.

Yet thirty years ago, if a budding Wall Street wizard had said, "I'm going to put your money into a company in an exacting, sophisticated business where five year olds with no discernible sense of taste or aesthetics will determine how adults spend billions of dollars," you'd have questioned their sanity. Today, you wouldn't think twice about accepting that recommendation.

McDonald's (and its various burger buddies) succeed day to day—with some of the most demanding customers on the face of the planet—because they have defined their competencies and built a specific combination of standards and style based on them that guides the way the company does business worldwide. FedEx, UPS, and other pacesetting delivery services have done the same thing in the delivery business. So have Ritz-Carlton, Marriott, Motel 6, and a host of competitors in the hotel business. As you begin, consciously and conscientiously, to do something similar, your brand will grow in strength and clarity in the eyes of others.

Clear, but in Context

Clarity is worth a little further exploration here. Life involves a certain amount of ambiguity. Too much precision, in fact, can be as bad as too little if it results in rigid, doctrinaire, lockstep responses to ever-changing needs. Strong brands, personal or business, tend to be defined by clear standards that prove consistently clear and meaningful over time.

You have your own definitions of both "fast" and "food" when you go to a burger barn, a convenience store, or a supermarket. The standards you expect each to adhere to have some common elements, but others will vary because they are uniquely appropriate to what each establishment is geared to provide. The same holds true with personal brands. The way we set and manage expectations around the strengths of our standards and style will help people relate to us effectively.

Time is a good example of how important it is to define and manage expectations in a relationship.

- Sometimes the importance of time can be based on clearly stated standards: next-day delivery service, for example, or a pre-arranged time for something (a movie, an airline flight, or a doctor's appointment) to start or end. You expect those standards to be adhered to, and you may be mildly to severely upset if they're not.

- Sometimes the time standard offers room to move. An important anniversary has a specific date on the calendar, but you might choose to celebrate it at eight in the morning or eight at night, which would probably affect the form of celebration.

- Some time values reflect a lasting impression from the past. Domino's no longer makes its "Thirty minutes or it's free" delivery promise (too much risk of litigation over young drivers running stop signs to make deliveries on time). But most people still expect the pizza delivery—no matter who's making it—to come close to that thirty-minute standard.

Because clear expectations help you judge how distinctive, relevant, and consistent a brand is for you, clarity is one hallmark of whether a brand is strong or weak. A strong brand stands for a very clear combination of roles, standards, and style, not just a vague approximation of what you can expect.

Not only is it important to set clear expectations, they also need to be maintained. The smallest and seemingly most insignificant things can have powerful consequences in the light of expected brand values.

Broken Window Syndrome

In recent years, many cities have become conscious of something called the "broken window syndrome." Often, when a building is abandoned, the first thing that happens is somebody breaks the windows. Those broken windows become a clue, an indicator to others that the property has become vulnerable.

If the windows are not repaired promptly, a predictable cycle of decline follows—vagrants move in, fires are started, plumbing fixtures are stolen, and so on. The cost of restoring the building to an acceptable quality level rises as its condition deteriorates, making it more likely that the slide into decline will spread to other properties nearby. Cities that use broken windows as an indicator of more serious problems to come intervene more quickly and proactively. The broken windows standard helps them do what they need to do in a more systematic and productive—hence competent—way.

What are the "broken windows" for your personal brand—the expected standards and style you're no longer meeting? They could be something as simple as phone calls not returned, birthdays not acknowledged, promises to attend a child's game or school event that somehow slide by unnoticed. Taken individually, none amounts to a major issue. But as individual instances solidify into habit patterns, the behavior becomes easier to continue, harder to redirect. And the people who are relating to your personal brand begin to modify their expectations of your standards.

Using Your Brand Dimensions

Brands reflect values—they are outward manifestations of what's inside of you. Those inner dimensions can be defined—and need to be—to build a brand for maximum impact. Now that you've identified them and linked them in your Personal Brand Dimensions Model, you have a powerful tool that can help you build a distinctively relevant and consistent brand. In turn, these dimensions can be used as a yardstick against which to measure yourself and make adjustments to keep yourself and your relationships on track.

Brands, like relationships, are experiential. That's another way of saying that brands build their strength over time, through interactions. The more distinctively relevant and consistent those interactions are, the faster and stronger our personal brands grow.

Unfortunately, most people don't spend much time thinking about the way the interactions in their lives play out. Consequently, their personal brands reflect a random pattern that sometimes succeeds and sometimes doesn't—and which often doesn't seem to respond to predictable norms. It shouldn't be surprising. Here's what that behavior looks like to the people evaluating the brand quality:

- There's no design for distinctiveness or relevancy in what they are trying to be in their relationship with someone else.
- There's no consistency in how they manage the interactions involved in that relationship.
- There's no promise of value at the heart of the relationship process.

That's why there's no strength in the brand relationship that results.

Your Brand Platform

As you look at your own Personal Brand Dimensions Model, what single driving force seems to energize it? If you asked the people who know you best to describe you in just a couple of words, what words or phrases would they come up with? This dominant brand value—either standard or style—is your brand platform.

Your brand platform is the single, most dominant characteristic of your brand—the one whose nature permeates everything else. In many ways it is what makes you distinctive. It must correlate with your most prized personal value. To determine your brand platform, review your list of brand standards and style characteristics and decide which of these you are most passionate about and have the courage to consistently and distinctly display—with everyone, all the time. Declaring your brand platform is an important step for developing your brand promise. In Chapter 6, we will provide you with a step-by-step process to develop your brand promise.

Now using the criteria mentioned here, write down your single-most important personal brand characteristic. My brand platform is:

_____

_____

To build a strong personal brand, you need to make a conscious effort to manage the relationships in your life so their interactions are memorable for all the right reasons: because they are a *distinctive* reflection of you, because they are *relevant* to someone else, and because they are *consistent* enough that both parties develop a sense of stability and predictability on which to build future interactions.

Now, how do you express the essence of that relationship in just a few words? You're now ready to use your personal brand dimensions and brand platform to work on your personal brand promise.

6 **Personal Brand Promise**

Making a Commitment to Your Brand

No one else can define what success means to you. Success can have as broad or narrow a definition as you choose. What your dreams and goals look and feel like today, tomorrow, or a year from now is very personal and unique to you. We make no judgments in that regard, for, as we've said, the most important brand relationship you have ultimately is with yourself. Therefore, building a strong personal brand is not just about being authentic to others. It is also—just as importantly—about being true to yourself.

Buddhism teaches the concept of "mindfulness." At the risk of greatly oversimplifying a very profound idea, we define mindfulness as the endeavor to be conscious and present as you move through each moment of your life. If you're being true to your personal brand, those choices will reflect the way you think, the way you feel, and the values with which you resonate.

But one fundamental choice is the primary influence on all other choices: every day you can choose consciously to move consistently, persistently, and boldly in the direction of your dreams. In other words, you can be conscious of what you want your life to be about (your purpose), what you want to achieve in your life (your vision), and what will guide your decisions (your values). By doing this, you are also aligning the most powerful forces at your disposal to help you build your own personal brand. Your purpose inspires you, your vision motivates you, and your values guide you.

With this sense of inner alignment in place, you can now learn how to manage your personal brand to achieve the results you want, and even to measure your progress realistically.

Achieving Brand Alignment

In business, a brand begins to build strength when the values of the organization and the values of its constituents are in alignment. Alignment leads to relationships that sustain themselves over the long term because both parties have common interests and are moving in the same direction. In the same way, when the values expressed in your personal brand align with belief systems held by the people who are important to you, stronger and more fulfilling personal relationships are created.

Brand Promise to Keep

In business, one way to determine the specific nature and usefulness of a product or service is by listening, however unconsciously, to its brand promise.

A brand promise is a statement that an organization (or an individual) uses internally *to focus its efforts on what its brand must deliver* externally *to satisfy needs in the real world.*

A personal brand promise is a way to state what you are committed to being for others. It helps you define how you want your decisions and actions to have a meaningful impact on someone else. Stating a brand promise helps you focus your efforts on what you must deliver to satisfy the needs of someone else in a relationship.

In business, a brand promise is often confused with slogans and taglines used to promote and market a brand. These may be the outward reminders of the promise, but they are not the promise itself. Rather, a brand promise is a commitment that businesses—and their people—make to their customers about what they are willing to do (and not do) on the customers' behalf. Usually, however, those promises are not expressed directly to the customers or other members of the public. They are generally kept private within the organization.

Every brand, including your personal brand, contains an implicit promise. Some are clearer than others. Some are more ambitious than others. Some are more appropriate than others. But a brand promise should reflect the desire and ability to meet another specific person's needs and desires at a particular time.

A brand promise shouldn't be made lightly, however. Nor should it be something that comes out differently in each different situation or relationship. Expressed well, it has applications across a broad spectrum. One very important personal brand management skill is learning to *apply* your brand promise to the specifics of each relationship, not to *change* it to suit a new situation. Essentially, you want to make a single brand promise to friends, family, and people at work. A true test of a personal brand promise statement is how well it connects to your brand platform and how you make it relevant to all the relationships in your life.

Making a brand promise is important. But *keeping* it is the real test. A statement of a brand promise is only a foundation for the brand. It then has to be tested—and either accepted or rejected—by the intended audience. In business, that means the organization's customers—the people who spend their money for what the business makes or does. On the personal side, it means the people with whom you are building relationships. Consider a familiar business example.

Helloooo, Federal

Think about FedEx for a moment. The FedEx brand promise is "An unrelenting commitment to deliver." As a customer, you may never have heard that promise stated in just those words. But if you're working for FedEx, whether sorting packages, driving a delivery truck, setting up airfreight schedules, or buying new computer systems, this promise provides a simple guide for your actions. It can lead to extraordinary responses.

Within FedEx, there are stories of drivers who have gone to amazing lengths to meet the company's delivery commitments—for example, picking up a locked drop box, concrete pedestal and all, to get the packages within it to the sorting center on time.

You can see that if everybody in a business organization lives out that kind of promise, customers will experience an unparalleled level of reliability. And because the people and systems of FedEx are geared for just this result, research consistently shows that the single most important service characteristic FedEx has emblazoned on the minds of customers is reliability. Consequently, "An unrelenting commitment to deliver" qualifies as a very relevant brand promise.

A promise can be an energizing component for a brand. But it doesn't exist in a vacuum. Whether—or how well—it connects to the people to whom it is made ultimately determines if the brand rises or falls. If a brand is a relationship, a successful brand is an *intimate* relationship. A business can promise its customers something they don't need or want or value. Even if it keeps that promise, it won't matter to them, and consequently the business won't obtain any competitive advantage from all its time and effort. Only when the promise connects to the important needs that lead the customers to value the relationship does keeping the promise generate real value for the brand.

The same holds true in a personal context. For the important people in your life, your brand promise sums up what you are committed to being and doing on their behalf. Because it needs to connect to the "real you" as well, it also reflects your values in meaningful ways that you can act upon. The brand promise you make to someone, however silently and implicitly, provides the energy that helps you consistently build distinctive, valuable relationships throughout your life.

A Platform for Promises

In Chapter 5, we used Jeannie Seeley-Smith to show you how to build your own brand dimensions. Jeannie is a prime example of a strong personal brand. Her completed personal brand manifesto appears in Appendix II.

Based on her particular combination of roles, standards, and style, compassion qualifies as Seeley-Smith's **brand platform**—the single most dominant characteristic of her brand, the one whose nature permeates everything else. She's realistic, enthusiastic, politically savvy, open to new ideas . . . but when it comes down to one key element that colors all the rest, her compassion comes to the fore. From it, we can distill her brand promise: "The insight to guide, the compassion to inspire." The key is that Jeannie's brand promise to others is built upon her brand platform—her strongest brand value.

There's no magic to creating effective personal brand promises. You'll know when you've got it right—you'll feel it. Start with your platform, then follow these quick guidelines:

- Effective brand promises should be short—five to eight words.
- They should be active, action-oriented, even exciting and inspirational.
- They should orient you directly or indirectly to how your brand pays off for someone else.
- They should be based on your most distinctive brand standard or brand style (your brand platform).

- They should reflect how your brand platform provides value to others.
- They should be fine-tuned through many iterations. Don't be reluctant to tinker and revise.
- They should eventually be extremely strong. Don't settle too soon: go for a great personal brand promise that will keep you motivated and focused on your brand strengths.
- They should be tested with close friends or family: if their eyes light up and they immediately sense how your promise can help you connect with others, it passes the test.

As models, consider these brand promises developed from the various personal brand examples throughout this book:

"Smart ideas put into action." (Jacque Rast—you'll meet her shortly)
"Do it right for the right reasons." (James Scothorn)
"Enthusiasm that will make your day." (Chip Bell)
"The insight to guide, the compassion to inspire." (Jeannie Seeley-Smith)

Your brand promise states how you will make a difference in relationships throughout your life. The key is knowing how to apply your brand promise in the different aspects of your life—work, marriage, partnerships, parenting, and more. Now, keeping in mind the guidelines on the previous page, write a brand promise. Remember to keep it concise. My brand promise is:

Targeting Your Brand Promise

Let's go back to the business side for a moment. FedEx's *competencies* center on getting packages to their destinations reliably and within a guaranteed amount of time. It has set *standards* in every facet of its organization to help demonstrate that competence to its customers. Over time, as a result, its customers have seen it deliver in a highly memorable style. From this combination of competencies, standards, and style, FedEx has created and continues to reinforce a perception of its brand in the minds of its customers.

FedEx has many different kinds of customers. Some want overnight delivery. Some specify second-day, even third-day, service. Some use the service only sporadically. Some use it so much that they've hired FedEx to serve as their parts warehouse, empowering the company to dispatch anything from tiny computer parts to large engine subassemblies whenever one of *their* customers calls.

To each, however, the FedEx brand promise remains the same: "An unrelenting commitment to deliver."

Note also how all three pieces of the Personal Brand Dimensions Model have to be in place for the brand itself to work:

- If the packages don't get where they're going, FedEx will be judged incompetent, and the relationship customers have with it will end right there.
- If its on-time delivery standard is met perhaps 95 percent of the time, or if about every sixth package comes through looking like it was handled by a gorilla, there will be no differentiation between FedEx's standards and countless other delivery services. (In other words, just getting it there isn't enough.)
- If the FedEx drivers who make pickups and deliveries are prone to snap at customers or thoughtlessly drive through the azaleas in front of the office, FedEx's "unrelenting commitment to deliver" won't have nearly the positive style aura that it has achieved since the company's founding in 1971.

Similar realities apply to personal brands. Relationships aren't created equal. Nor do they all make the same claim on you. Among the many categories of relationships you have, some have a higher priority—and payoff—and thus persuade you to focus specific efforts to strengthen them. Nonetheless, the test of a good brand promise is whether it can be applied across a broad spectrum of relationships.

What FedEx does, consciously and unconsciously, you can do, too. Developing an effective brand promise will be one of the most important things you do to make your personal brand powerful. When they're on target, brand promises come to serve as internal mantras—quiet metronomes that keep you conscious of what you consistently need to do to make your brand come alive and stay alive.

Making It Personal

As we've seen, relationships often develop around our perceived competence to interact with someone: a spouse, customer, friend, or coworker. The promises we make in each of these different situations will be essentially the same. We'll modify our behavior as appropriate to deliver on them in each instance, but through all the various relationship encounters we have, we'll constantly return to a common foundation—our brand promise.

Your Brand Promise at Work

Organizations exist for many purposes—to provide products, deliver services, create employment, and enliven communities, to name just a few. Those who work for the organization are hired for their ability to help carry out these missions. The quality of service different people provide, however, is an infinitely variable reflection of how clear and committed they are as employees to that sense of mission.

Sadly, far too many people cannot answer the question, Why are you here? or What is the purpose of *your* job? in terms that would be meaningful to their customers, their colleagues, or their employers. This lack of clarity affects their motivation and productivity, and thus costs both them and the organization that employs them dearly. On the other hand, when the purpose and importance of a person's work is clear to the individual *and* recognized and reinforced by the organization, magic happens. Morale skyrockets. Relationships deepen and grow. Customers notice.

One of the most inspiring and meaningful ways you can express your purpose at work is through the promise you make, however silently, to your customers, your colleagues, and the company at large. In this context, your brand promise not only provides a constant touchstone for your actions but also becomes the criterion by which you can judge the success of your efforts. Should you face moments of doubt or indecision, you can look to this promise and ask, Are my actions and decisions helping me keep my promise, or are they hindering me from doing so?

Being clear about your brand promise also reminds you why your work is important and what your responsibilities are to other members of your team. To better apply your brand promise at work, consider:

- What are the key relationships in your working life? The "customers" for your brand at work are those who are most affected by the quality of your work.
- What do these people expect of me? Your actions, and the outcomes that result, are especially relevant in the context of these relationships.
- How can I apply my brand promise so that I am both distinctive and relevant in these relationships? Think of situations where you can clearly demonstrate your brand promise to make a real impact.

Someone whose name is sure to come up when Karl is offering examples of brand promises in a work context is Jacque Rast. Jacque has been able to succeed in the traditionally male-dominated world of engineering, working her way up through an industry-leading firm and now running her own business, by applying a very keen mind in a straight-forward, action-oriented manner. Her personal brand promise of "smart ideas put into action" is evident and respected in all of her relationships. Her personal brand manifesto is shown on the next page.

At work and at home, Jacque's brand standards (including smart, marketing savvy, and results-oriented) and her brand style (professional, caring, and outgoing, among other attributes) consistently come through. And they've been coming through for many years now. No client of Karl's—especially none from outside the field of marketing—ever learned the concepts of brand management faster. Jacque Rast has been able to apply these concepts first at a global-leading engineering consulting firm, subsequently as cofounder (with her husband, Richard) of Talisman Partners, a Denver-based environmental information services and consulting firm.

This is no small feat—especially in a field steeped in traditional thinking about marketing. By demonstrating consistent results, Jacque was able to gain the confidence and conviction of senior management at her previous firm, building support for brand management as a core business strategy. She continually put "smart ideas into action," integrating her ideas with the needs of the firm's customers to produce results that guaranteed her contributions would be woven into the day-to-day business style of the organization, not simply discarded. If she'd had less savvy or less ability to implement her ideas, they'd have seemed like just another pointless marketing communications activity sent down from headquarters.

As a top executive of Talisman, she continues to impress clients with her ability to cut quickly to the heart of a situation and to provide immediate, smart analysis of possible response scenarios. Her knowledge of, and dedication to, brand management encourages Talisman's employees to live the brand they see embodied every day in their CEO.

Jacque's brand approach carries over to her personal life as well: the same quick, smart thinking goes into everything from sorting out

PERSONAL BRAND MANIFESTO

Personal Brand Dimensions for
Jacque Rast

* Environmental
  Engineer
* Business
  Owner
* Wife
* Stepmom

Roles
Our relationship
with others

Standards
How we do it

BRAND

Style
How we relate
to others

* Smart
* Marketing
  Savvy
* Results-
  Oriented
* Innovative
* Thorough

* Professional
* Outgoing
* Caring

Personal Brand Platform: Smart—Brand Standard

Personal Brand Promise: "Smart ideas put into action."

scheduling opportunities with her stepsons to her approaches to downhill skiing and gardening. Whatever she's doing, it reflects a commitment to "smart ideas put into action."

Your Brand Promise to a Spouse or Life Partner

For most people, being loved, valued, and appreciated by a spouse or life partner—and loving, valuing, and appreciating in return—are benefits they hope to experience in one exceptional relationship in their lives. If and when they have an opportunity to create that kind of special relationship, success will not be achieved simply by sticking around. It will only be earned by two people who are willing to learn and grow together in a relationship characterized by the utmost respect and concern for each other's well-being. With that in mind, reflect on the following questions:

- What attracts me to this person? What are the affinities between us? Do they spring from similar ideas about purpose, vision, and values? Very likely they do.
- What does this person expect of me? What attitudes and behaviors do they want from me? How am I relevant to this person?
- How can I apply my brand promise so that I am both distinctive and relevant in this particular relationship? Think of situations where you can clearly demonstrate your brand promise to make a real impact on this relationship.

The answers to these questions can help you discover what your spouse or partner wants from you, which can guide you in applying your brand promise in a manner that is meaningful to both them and you.

Your Brand Promise as a Parent

Parenting today is an area of great vulnerability. Changing work styles and lifestyles have created significant, often heated discussions on the appropriate and "correct" way to parent. We believe that the methodologies of successful parenting can be as varied as the personalities of the parents. But if the outcome each person desires to achieve as a parent is summed up as a dedication to raising healthy children (in the broadest sense), then most parents are after the same thing.

Reflecting on how you would apply your promise as a parent might lead you to ask,

- Where in childhood are my children now, and what stage are they moving to? At different ages and in different settings, children need different things from their parents. It's not a lockstep, changeless role you're called on to play.

- What in particular do they expect of me? Your role may be modified by the presence or absence of another parent, or the network of an extended family, or support (or threats) from the surrounding community.
- How can I remain both distinctive and relevant in these relationships? Committed parents are prepared to adjust their responses to other demands to make sure their children receive the time, affection, lessons, and support they require. Yet they also recognize the need to balance that response in the context of the other roles they play, as income-earner, life partner, friend, and—it needs to be affirmed—as a whole and complete individual.

Your Brand Promise as a Friend

Many people find friendship to be one of their most valued privileges. True friends can provide us with genuine compassion in dark times, celebrate our achievements without envy, and laugh at our foibles and eccentricities as we laugh at theirs. One special aspect of friendship (also true of the bond between spouses or life partners) is the fact that friends are connected by conscious choice, not by accidents of birth or workplace proximity.

Friendships can reach even deeper and more meaningful levels when people learn how to apply their brand promise in these relationships. Ask yourself,

- Whom do I regard as my closest friends? Name names: identifying these individuals will provide insight into their needs and their importance to your life.
- What do they expect of me? Perhaps no kind of relationship in your life will be characterized by more diverse needs and profiles. This makes looking at each one especially important.

- How do I keep on being both distinctive and relevant in these relationships? Think of situations where you can make a real impact by acting on your brand promise.

Moving beyond Brand Basics

A strong personal brand stands for something. The more clearly defined your brand becomes, the more authentic, lasting, and rewarding the relationships built on it are likely to be. People will see you for who you are, warts and all—but they will see you more clearly and relate to you more effectively as a result of the clarity a well-defined brand brings to a relationship.

On that basis, we're now ready to introduce you to some "advanced branding"—ways to build depth, breadth, and perspective as you work at creating, enhancing, and constantly refining your personal brand.

7 Personal Brand Strategies

Measuring and Strengthening Your Brand

Once you've identified and completed your brand manifesto and articulated a brand promise, you've established an excellent foundation for building a strong personal brand. But that effort will be significantly depleted unless you develop systematic ways to make sure that first, you are indeed making distinctive, relevant, and consistent connections to the important people in your life; and second, what you're delivering is truly valued by the other person in each relationship. That feedback, in turn, helps you further define your objectives, refine your strategies, and manage your actions.

Building Brand Equity

This brings us to the concept of **brand equity.** A brand relationship is like a bank account. When something strengthens the relationship, you're effectively making a deposit. When things consistently strengthen the relationship, the balance grows—and accrues interest.

Brands are like that. Successful interactions build the expectation that things will go right the next time, too. If they do, brand equity continues to grow. When something goes wrong, on the other hand, the equity in the brand account is tapped and reduced. If the account is well into the black, even major problems can be encountered and survived without destroying the relationship. But if the balance goes into the red, the relationship can be irrevocably broken.

Karl has worked with a number of organizations in the express delivery business, like FedEx and the U.S. Postal Service. Both have the same basic competencies—they deliver packages and letters. But the very different standards and styles they bring to the effort have a tremendous impact.

If FedEx misses a delivery time, research indicates their customers are upset, but not violently so. The company's brand image for reliability—which it has built delivery by delivery over many years— reassures temporarily disappointed customers that such performance is not normal and, in the long run, won't be acceptable to FedEx any more than it is to them.

On the other hand, when the U.S. Postal Service misses on a commitment, even by just a little bit, research shows that its customers (many of whom are also customers of FedEx, UPS, and other more time-driven delivery services) are less tolerant. They're more likely to become enraged and quicker to ask for their money back. Even though the Postal Service provides an uncommon level of service *most of the time,* years of lackluster performance and neglect have burned off a lot of the goodwill it might otherwise be able to fall back on.

That's why it's so important to pay attention to the standards and style people expect to be an integral part of the relationship. According to a common business rule of thumb, seven things must go right to make up for one thing that goes wrong. Small wonder that, time and again, consistency—of behavior, of performance, of experience, and of expectations—turns out to be the key factor in determining whether a brand develops the strength and staying power to survive and thrive over the longer term. That's what makes your brand promises, stated or implied, credible or incredible to others.

Brands That Last

In the context of business, we sometimes say that you know a brand by its extremes: you really get to know what a brand represents in the worst of times and the best of times—how things are done when everything's on a roll and what happens under duress. Both ends of the spectrum provide an opportunity for a brand to demonstrate its true mettle. And both have a significant effect on the balance in the brand equity account.

The first time a personal relationship provides value for someone else, brand equity starts to accrue. As the cycle repeats, the relationship grows stronger, more resilient, and less vulnerable to the forces that can conspire to pull people apart. John Grisham's novel *The Firm* (Doubleday, 1991) and the movie version starring Tom Cruise tell the story of an idealistic young lawyer who is led astray by his dishonest partners and the lavish lifestyle they heap upon him. His new wife finally leaves him when he betrays the common values that brought them together. At the end of the movie, however, his true values win, and the wife tells her husband why she came back to him: "You kept your promise." Amid all the uproar the dishonest partners could contrive, the main character's strong personal brand lived up to its brand promise of integrity and respect for the law.

As a relationship demonstrates its value over time, a level of loyalty can be created that can withstand even the worst of times. The equity you build up through being distinctive, relevant, and consistent provides a safety net when circumstances conspire against you. But nothing lasts forever. Overdraw the brand equity account, and even the most brand-loyal customer will finally reach a point when their relationship with you no longer has value. It has lost its relevance. It has become distinctively inconsistent. At that point, it's over.

Think about the emotional nastiness that so often attends a divorce, a firing, or a messy breakup. Anger. Frustration. Bitterness.

Despair. Huge emotional swings. The destruction of a once strong brand relationship reflects the depth and strength that once was the norm. The very things that once made the relationship strong collapse into and add to the emotional rubble when the relationship fails.

We understand why some people become "relationship-shy"— wary of trying to build another intimate personal or professional relationship. Too often, they've built only to see the structure give way and fall. The Personal Brand Dimensions Model can help you improve your odds of building something lasting.

If you look around, you know which people in your life you count on, come what may. You may never have thought of that as evidence of a strong personal brand before, but by now you should be beginning to see patterns. You may even find you know someone well enough to sketch out their personal brand manifesto.

The people you count on have proven themselves consistently and distinctively relevant to you in a specific set of circumstances. You know what you can turn to them for, and you have a pretty good idea of how they'll respond. That's a branded relationship.

A Word about Transactions

To measure the way people interact with your personal brand, you will need to identify the variables involved. Len Berry, author of *Discovering the Soul of Service* (The Free Press, 1999), developed a three-part equation that can help. He notes that in every transaction, participants have three different perspectives from which to judge what is happening:

1. They have their *expectations* of what will happen.
2. They have their *experiences* of what did happen.
3. They have their *observations* of the process of getting from expectations to experience.

All three are important. But in Berry's view, an interesting compounding effect also needs to be taken into account. Rather than simply being added together, Berry's three variables multiply each other. In other words, it's not 1 + 2 + 3 that determines how well you're doing but 1 x 2 x 3. Remember, when you multiply something by zero in an equation, the total goes to zero no matter how large the other variables might be.

As Berry's little formula helps explain, everything counts in a relationship. You can go to the doctor and receive competent medical care, but if you notice dirt under his fingernails or her office has a funny smell to it, you start wondering about standards and style. Your observations of the process could keep you from going back and renewing that relationship, no matter how prestigious the name of the medical school on the diploma hanging on the wall. One variable goes to zero and everything zeroes out.

Measuring as a Process

The best businesses measure constantly, and they probe all three areas. In particular, they know how often perception defines reality in our world—what people *think* they see is what they *think* they are getting. Consequently, businesses focus a lot of their research efforts on comparing what their customers perceive to what the business wants them to perceive (the intended "reality" of the brand) and also on looking for gaps between perception and reality. Closing those gaps, they've learned, is crucial to long-term satisfaction and staying power. Synchronizing perception with reality becomes a significant focal point for brand-management efforts and justifies doing regular measurement often.

The questions businesses use in brand measurement are wide-ranging. Is the product creating an image—together with an emotional connection—in the customer's mind? If so, are the image and connection the ones the business intends, or something else? Can they be sustained? Is the brand undervalued? Is it overvalued? Is it being confused with competing alternatives?

All of these questions can apply in a personal context. Suppose you have decided that a key piece of your personal brand promise—remember, consistency should apply in all your important relationships—is that you will always be available and will listen to key people in your life. When you start measuring, you'll want to find out whether that's something they value. More importantly, do they act as if they believe you will deliver on that promise?

Check the data you are receiving from your own observations. If they think you are there to listen, your children or coworkers will make an effort to communicate with you. And it will be more than surface chatter: they might (to a degree they consider appropriate and valuable) confide in you, or seek your opinions, or ask for guidance. Are they doing these things? If not, you need to probe to find out why not.

Bottom line: Remember, everyone has a brand. We're looking at how accurately your brand reflects your values in the minds of other people who are important to you. You must constantly measure your brand to understand what it stands for and how it is impacting relationships in your life.

Ask Around

If the relationship is important, then it's worth managing deliberately rather than by happenstance. Just from your own day-to-day observations, you can begin to develop a sense of whether people are experiencing the brand you are seeking to create.

But don't settle for a single data source—and a subjective one at that. The observations of people you know and trust (spouses, friends, and others) can help you fill in the picture in more detail. Take full advantage of their perspectives on a regular basis. Ask them what they're seeing, and combine their observations with your own to further guide your brand-building efforts.

Think of it as a form of navigation. Whether you're in a canoe or on a cruise ship, a basic principle of knowing where you are on the water is to choose and steer by significant, reliable landmarks. Taking constant sightings on them helps you to stay on course. The more prominent and readily identifiable your landmarks, the easier it is to navigate. The more often you check your landmarks, the smaller your course corrections will need to be and the greater the likelihood you'll reach your destination in a quick, productive, and orderly way.

If you continually check the status of your personal brand relationships (without making a pest of yourself, of course), you will discover how you're doing at reaching your objectives. If you're on target, you will begin to compile "anecdotal evidence" that (to use the earlier listening example) your children or colleagues are indeed using you as a sounding board—asking for and acting on your insights about what they do, where they go, the dreams they have, and the issues they face.

If there's a gap, on the other hand, where is it coming from?

It could be you. Despite your brand promise to be available and listen, how often are you actually in a physical and mental state where you can give your full attention to someone else? Are you exhausted from other demands? Are you habitually behind the barrier of the newspaper (or the computer), or asleep in front of the television, or so involved in other activities that they don't think you have time for them?

It could also be them. Are they able to take advantage of the brand promise you're prepared to make on their behalf? Are they even aware of it? Maybe they're not comfortable confiding in anyone at this point. Or maybe they just haven't received any indication from you that listening is something you're prepared to do and good at doing. People may be surprised to learn you aspire to be seen as a helpful, supportive listener, which is an example of why "customer education" is such an important part of building productive brand expectations.

Seek Consistency

When you're paddling a canoe, you'd be well advised to look up and around constantly. Whenever a gap opens up between where you're going and where you want to be going, the sooner you spot the deviation, the quicker you can correct your course—and the less radical your adjustments will need to be. Brand measurement works the same way. Use your observations and the feedback you're receiving from trustworthy sources to look for gaps and progress points. Then work systematically to close the gaps. The more consistent you are at staying on course, the more quickly you'll get where you want to go.

Inconsistency is the devil of a strong brand. If listening is a key brand standard for you, make sure your children or workplace colleagues see you model the behavior of being available and an open listener with others. Respect the confidences of those who confide in you. If people experience adverse consequences when they take you into their confidence, that might lead someone else to think you will react more as a judge, a critic, or a malicious gossip than as a constructive coach or a guide.

Consistency cuts both ways. If you are inconsistent, people—even people very close to you, whom you think should know you better—may not feel they know who you are or what you will do. If they can't count on consistent behavior, if they have to wonder about what you will do in ordinary circumstances, they will find it hard to trust you when the chips are really down, no matter how often or articulately you promise something.

Since actions speak louder than words, if your actions are inconsistent with your words, people will quickly learn to discount your promises. When you truly walk the same path you talk and deliver on the promises you make, they learn to trust you, value you, and count on you to be there for them in the future. Your brand starts to stand for something in their eyes.

Indirect Measurement Tools

Businesses have learned to combine direct and indirect brand-evaluation techniques to build a more accurate picture of the effectiveness of their brand messages. Here are a few indirect measurement tools and some ideas on how you can apply them to keep your personal brand relationships on track.

How far will people go to offer feedback or ideas, including suggestions for improving a brand? A customer who writes to a company about a valued product or service experience is providing evidence of a deeper relationship than someone who checks off a couple of boxes on a handy comment card. Both are placing more value on the relationship than customers (however satisfied they may profess to be) who don't consider it worthwhile to invest the time and energy to offer any feedback at all.

When someone takes the time to tell you what they like—and what they would like even more—they're making their own investment in furthering the relationship. Pay attention to praise, compliments, and other positive feedback. They are evidence that people are giving you credit for a brand strength, something they value and would like to see continue.

What kinds of complaints do people have—and give voice to? In pacesetting organizations, a complaining customer, far from being seen as a nuisance, is considered an invaluable resource for product, service, and process improvement. Research suggests that only four percent of customers who have a complaint will actually register it. For every customer who speaks up, another twenty-four suffer in silence—and probably are already looking for new brand relationships. (Meanwhile, they're telling all their friends what a poor job your organization did for them.)

When someone takes the time to let you know you've come up short on your brand promise, use it as a valuable opportunity to retarget your efforts. But remember to examine both sides of the relationship to see where the disconnect originates. Maybe you promised more than you could—or did—deliver, which means you need to focus on consistency. But maybe the intended recipient expected something other than what you actually promised, which means you need to redefine expectations with them. In either case, constructive criticism can help you fine-tune your game.

What are customers willing to do for a brand? A business might ask, If a unit of Brand Us fell off the shelf at Target, Nordstrom, or Barnes & Noble, would a customer pick it up? The response reveals interesting things about the way people perceive a brand's quality (or lack thereof).

What are people willing to do for your personal brand? Do they return your calls? Do they provide feedback or advance information? Will they add an errand of yours to their to-do list? If a memo or magazine for you was misdirected, would they personally drop it by? Similarly, think about the relationships in which you consistently are willing to go "above and beyond," and ask yourself what that reveals about someone else's strong personal brand relationship with you.

What things do people tell others about the brand? In business, the most powerful form of advertising is word-of-mouth. That's why testimonials are such staples of brand communications activities and why referrals are so highly prized by well-run businesses. Here's a demonstration of how relationship values affect credibility. Researchers have learned that people may say one thing but do something else when the question is phrased to involve just *their* behavior. But when the question probes the individual's willingness (or unwillingness) to recommend something to a *friend*, the reliability of the response goes up—as it should, because now they're being asked to react on the basis of a relationship.

When someone comes to you on the recommendation of someone else, find out who sent them—and why. (And remember to thank the referring individual when an opportunity presents itself.) Make sure they bring realistic expectations; and make sure you meet them or revise them as necessary, because two brand relationships are involved here: the one they're starting to build with you *and* the one they already have with whomever sent them to you.

In this vein, listen to the word-of-mouth you pass along to others. How do you describe people you respect, like, and admire, compared to those who don't rate high on your value scale (and what does the tone of your opinions say about your own brand)? What about their personal brands has or hasn't made an impression on you—and what lessons can you learn from your observations that can be applied to your own personal branding efforts?

Brand Management Tools

Beyond measurement techniques, businesses use a variety of tools to define, manage, and extend a brand. Many of them can be adapted to the needs of a strong personal brand as well.

Guidelines: Businesses often create—and measure—specific standards and usage guidelines to help people stay true to a brand's values in day-to-day decision making. Your brand manifesto can serve as a similar "bible" for your brand. In fact, you might want to put your brand manifesto on a card and carry it with you.

Take a moment to write out some of the standards and guidelines that can strengthen the way your brand is perceived. These may involve the way you dress, the way you speak, how you show interest in others, or a host of other behaviors. Try to keep your list focused on creating a distinctive, relevant, and consistent brand impression.

_____

_____

_____

_____

Remember, little things count a lot. Jim Miller, coauthor of *The Corporate Coach* (HarperBusiness, 1994), was known around the Texas office-supply company he founded for the simple word "terrific." His brand guidelines were so thorough he had even thought through how he would respond to the way people greeted him. Whenever someone, in even the most casual of contexts, asked him how he was doing, he'd never sigh and say, "Oh, fine." He'd immediately reply, "I'm terrific—how are you?" Small wonder he was well known, not just in his company but throughout the entire office-products industry, for a powerful positive outlook that defined his strong personal brand.

Training: A proven way to improve what you do is to improve yourself. Yet often, in the hustle and bustle of daily life, self-improvement efforts go to the bottom of the to-do list. Experience is a good teacher, it's true, but the personal equivalent of learning on the job is often a traumatic way to figure something out. Businesses often set a target (sometimes measured in hours, sometimes in courses or certifications or continuing education units) for personal and professional improvement activities. In doing so, they further emphasize their belief that people will become more productive as a result of a regular learning regimen.

Are you willing and able to invest in improving yourself? The two basics are time and money. If you want to improve your parenting, listening, or computer skills, buy a book and make the time to read up on the subject. Lay a foundation for new interests or extend current ones by taking a class at a local college or through community education. On a less formal but equally forward-looking level, try to put yourself in situations where you can practice desired skills and gain useful experience that can be used in other relationships. Volunteer your time and talents at school, in the community, around the neighborhood, with your extended family—but do so with a purpose.

Special Events: Many normal, everyday business efforts are punctuated by special activities—sales, promotions, event sponsorships, and the like—that gain force because they are, by definition, out of the ordinary. Their rarity adds to their significance and impact, not to mention the organization's visibility. Businesses use these opportunities to go out of their way to create special focus on brand dynamics.

Can you reinforce and extend some of your own personal brand values in a similar fashion? Perhaps in the way you celebrate an anniversary or special day in a relationship? Perhaps through public involvement (volunteer work, community leadership, or assisting at school or with the elderly) that reflects a core personal value? Perhaps just making a deliberate point of saying "thanks" or "well done," or telling someone what they've done to please you? The event doesn't have to be special to become special to someone else. And celebrating it reinforces the value you place on your relationships.

Reward and Recognition: One of the oldest and most true axioms of business is "What gets rewarded gets repeated." Reinforcing small, ordinary positive behaviors and desired results is every bit as important—*more* important, in fact—than attacking areas where someone may not always measure up. It's also more useful than going overboard celebrating exceptional performance that, by its very nature, is never going to be the norm.

Behavioral psychologists say that to be clearly perceived as a positive rather than a negative individual you need to make at least three times as many upbeat remarks as negative comments. What's your ratio? If more than one-quarter of your comments are critical, complaining, or corrective—no matter how well-intended or needed your responses may be—you're going to be perceived negatively rather than positively. If you want your children, coworkers, or friends to value you for your positive contributions, they need to see your positive side in action far more often than the critical side.

Building a strong brand takes time. It involves work. It's an evolutionary process, not a one-time event—as befits the essential nature of a relationship. Don't take things for granted. Question, probe, evaluate, challenge. Then continually improve to build both the strength of your personal brand and the strength of the relationships people develop with it. And with you.

8 | Sign Up or Sign Out

Aligning with Your Employer's Brand

If there's one place more than any other where the idea of personal (as opposed to business) branding will be put to its greatest test, it's in the environment in which the two worlds combine, and occasionally collide—the workplace.

Our Life's Work

Most of us spend a large percentage of our time working. In fact, people relate so strongly to what they do that when they describe themselves, it is very often in terms of their work:

"I'm a doctor."

"I'm a manager."

"I'm in sales."

"I'm a teacher."

"I'm a housewife."

"I run a small business."

"I'm in business for myself."

Whether you're salaried, work by the hour, own the enterprise, have a fancy title or not, the purpose of your work is to create value—for yourselves and for others—in both tangible and intangible ways. When you and your employer understand that purpose, an opportunity for dynamic synergy between your personal brand and their business brand is created.

In other words, when the values you stand for and the values your organization stands for align, magic happens. Individuals have more opportunities and a greater desire to succeed because they are working in an environment that encourages them to be more of who they are, not less. Organizations get more highly committed workers. When your personal values are in harmony with your employer's, you see the success of your employer's brand as the successful expression of your own brand.

All brands are experiential—their strengths grow based on constant interactions. Just as the experiences customers have with a business brand shape their perceptions of it, and the experiences people have with you build an impression of your personal brand, the experiences you have on the job create a similar sense of an employer's brand. In the best of circumstances, your values and those of your employer will not only be compatible but will also combine in the best interests of the organization's customers. The more alignment among the three, the greater the synergy involved. When all three relationships align, powerful things happen.

For many people, however, such perfect alignment is more a matter of wishful thinking than day-to-day reality. They approach work as, well, work—just a job to be endured rather than an experience to be enjoyed. Small wonder so many customers pronounce themselves dissatisfied with what they experience from the businesses with which they interact.

Multiple Brand Dynamics

Now that you have a sense for how brands develop and how they can be consciously built to better align with the needs of others, you have a tool kit for gleaning insights into how to make the most of your relationship with your employer. Developing a personal brand won't magically make on-the-job conflicts go away. It can't. But it can help you clarify where your values and those of your employer are in harmony and where they are in conflict. That clarity will enable you to make informed decisions about what you're prepared to do and what you basically cannot do as you devote your personal time and energy to the world of work.

You may not be alone in this regard. Increasingly, successful businesses are beginning to recognize that just as their products and services develop—and ultimately profit from—brand relationships with their customers, the business itself can consciously develop a brand relationship with its employees. Even if your employer is not working deliberately toward this goal, as your brand awareness grows, you should find it progressively easier to define this relationship. In the process, you may be able to cut through some of the minor irritants that plague any workplace.

A Lot of "Bull"

Karl has watched this concept of brand alignment at work in his consulting work with Cargill, the global agribusiness leader. In its nutrition division, a vibrant internal case study has been built around a young woman in Texas who used the company's feed to raise a championship bull. The brand value discussion doesn't focus on her winning a blue ribbon. That's just a symbol. As the story unfolds, Cargill employees begin to see that the real payoff is in the pride she felt, the added self-confidence she now displays, and the experiences that will serve her all her life.

For Cargill, the power in the story comes from the lesson its people learned and took to heart: "Because of our high-quality feed and timely advice, our customer was able to be successful. We did that.

We're not just selling bags of cattle feed. We're helping young people learn the skills, hard work, and self-confidence it takes to become champions."

Anecdotally, similar employer brand-building stories can be found in all kinds of organizations:

- At Medtronic, a variety of meetings—from sales conferences to the annual shareholder gathering—feature live and videotaped "visits" from people who are alive today because of the company's heart pacemakers. Employees understand and firmly believe in Medtronic's commitment to humankind, reflected in the company's tagline "When life depends upon medical technology."

- At FedEx, people are encouraged to focus not on boxes and envelopes but on their contents—and the fact that someone somewhere may find them vitally important. ("I don't just sort packages. I make sure someone receives something they urgently need, absolutely, positively on time.")

- Leadership development activities at Alcoa are built around the organization's defined set of values and the way it implements them in global markets. ("I don't just account for so many tons of metals. I help people create the materials that improve someone's quality of life.")

- As anyone knows who has swung a hammer or wielded a paintbrush for organizations such as Habitat for Humanity, the real point of the exercise is the people, not the process. ("It's not just a house. It's a home for someone who wouldn't otherwise own a home if I hadn't helped.")

In every case above, the objective of work itself becomes more visible—and more valued. When we lift our focus from the *thing* we're making or doing to the *person* for whom we're making or doing it, the true meaning of work comes to light. As a consequence, we are fulfilled.

Above and Beyond

It would be wonderful if all working relationships would resonate with such values. Maybe someday they will. Meanwhile, it's worth noting that sometimes the "problem" is less a matter of conflicting values and more a matter of irritants that, placed in proper context, shrink to much more manageable dimensions.

A number of years ago, David counseled an airline mechanic on just such a values quandary. "Alex" (at his request, not his real name) had four children and the inevitable expenses of such a large family. Alex also worked for a company and in an environment that appeared to have very little in common with his personal values.

Some things that went on, or failed to go on, at work had come to grate constantly on his nerves. He felt no support, no recognition, yet heard plenty of unpleasant gossip. He thought about quitting, but his wages and benefits were providing vital financial security for his family—much more security, he knew, than he could earn elsewhere. Because his roles of husband and father were of the utmost importance to him, Alex felt trapped.

David and Alex discussed Alex's sense of purpose, his vision for his life, and the values that were most important to him. Gradually, he came to see that his work—and the benefits it provided for his family—aligned well with his sense of purpose. He also realized that there was no shortage of opportunities with his employer—how far he went was entirely up to him. And, the really good news was that he did believe in what he was doing.

David helped Alex make a deep connection with the fact that every person on every airplane that he took care of was depending on him to use all of his skills on their behalf. Alex also realized that the airline was as committed to the safety of its passengers as Alex was .

With that understanding, David and Alex turned to specific analysis of relationships on the job. Starting with himself, Alex examined whether or not his discomfort at work was related to a conflict between his values and that of the organization or whether it was just some individuals who got his goat. Alex realized it was the latter, for at no time did his employer force him to compromise his values or his sense of doing his job well.

In that light, Alex began to see that irritating people exist in every work environment and decided that they were bearable for three reasons. First, these relationships didn't call into question his essential competence as a mechanic. Second, no one was pushing him to send planes out of the hangar in an unsafe condition—in fact, safety was the number one value of his employer. Finally, in spite of whatever interpersonal conflict and lack of recognition he experienced, Alex was better able to fulfill his responsibilities to his family at his current job than if he quit and looked for a job elsewhere, where the salary and benefits would probably be much less.

Linking with Your Employer's Brand

The power of brand building lies in aligning the values between a brand and its customers. That emotional connection ignites brand loyalty. Every savvy business executive knows that great brands get their strength from inside the organization. Brand loyalty starts with the linkage between the values of the employees and the employer. If you clearly understood, or even had to develop, your employer's brand manifesto (better known as a brand strategy in the business world), then laid it beside your personal brand manifesto, how similar or dissimilar would they be? Your values and those of your employer don't have to match exactly, but they should align in key places. In that sense, the comparison may help to clarify some basic understandings. Whom do you do your work for? Whose life is improved because of what you do and how you do it?

- Do you push papers or expedite the information that improves *someone*'s life?
- Do you clean rooms (dishes, buildings, computer databases, etc.) or give *someone* a nicer, cleaner, healthier, better environment in which to live or work?
- Do you work with words or numbers, or help *someone* make better sense of their world?

Not only that, but how far do the ripple effects spread as your efforts, in turn, allow someone else to do something for someone, and so on outward from the source? Stopping and thinking about where your work goes and to whom it's important can make all the difference between feeling powerful or powerless, productive or pointless, invaluable or invisible.

In the preceding chapters, you've picked up a lot of useful brand analysis tools. Now is the time to use them to define your employer's brand and determine how closely it aligns with your own. There are two ways to go about the first task. The easiest way is to obtain a copy of your employer's brand strategy. If your employer has not documented a brand strategy, which would not be a rare occurrence, then you will have to surmise one on your own. Of course, there is always the possibility that you are not allowed access to the company's existing brand strategy. If your employer has not documented a brand strategy or you are not allowed access to it, you will have to surmise one on your own.

Let's first focus on determining if your employer already has a documented brand strategy. Let's be clear on what you're looking for. Different companies may call a brand strategy by different names, such as "corporate brand strategy," "corporate identity strategy," "positioning strategy," or "corporate identity guidelines." You may find the brand strategy in one or more of a few different places. Search your employer's intranet site under the corporate identity or brand strategy sections. Another approach is to call or email the corporate communications department and ask them for a copy. If your search is going slowly, ask someone in the marketing department to provide you with some clues to find your employer's brand strategy.

When you find the brand strategy, look for a statement of **core values** and a **brand promise** statement. If there is no brand promise statement, you will have to substitute the brand positioning statement. Do not look for a tag line or advertising theme. Tag lines and advertising slogans change often, don't always reflect the values inherent in the employer brand, and are designed as "catch phrases" to grab the attention of consumers.

If you are lucky enough to work for an employer who has a brand strategy and gives you access to it, you can begin the process of looking for alignment between your personal brand and your employer's brand. However, if you have not been able to gain access to your employer's core values and brand promise, you will need to estimate or surmise the brand values of the organization. The following process will take a bit of work on your part, but when it is successful, it will provide you with the information you need to compare your personal brand values with the brand values of your employer.

- If you don't have a copy of your organization's core values, ask your supervisor or the human resources department. Most companies will have a published set of core values. Now compare the statement of core values with the real-world "working values." By working values, we mean the values that are reflected in the way employees (managers and coworkers) interact with each other on a day-to-day basis—the real values that run through the organization. Make a list of the real values that you hold to be true in your organization.
- What are your organization's competencies? What standards

does it bring to those competencies? What style? Go through the process outlined in Chapter 5 to define your employer's brand dimensions. Remember, list only the dimensions that are distinctive and consistent in the way the organization interacts with its customers. Brand dimensions can be positive or negative.

- What is your employer's brand promise? Use your employer's brand dimensions as a starting point and follow the process outlined in Chapter 6 to derive a brand promise.

Now begin the process of checking for alignment between your personal brand manifesto and your employer's brand strategy. Compare values, brand dimensions, and brand promises. Where do they align and where do they contradict each other? There is no magic to this process. The more alignment the better. Don't expect perfect alignment, but an alarm should go off if you find none. Take special note of the values that do align. These areas become keystones where you are relevant to your employer and, therefore, ongoing opportunities for you to demonstrate the linkage with your employer's brand values and be distinctive in the employee/employer relationship.

A Provocative Premise

We started this chapter under a deliberately stark title. We think it concisely summarizes the basic challenge facing you, wherever your workplace may be. You can "sign up"—decide that you're in the right place and doing the right things for the right kind of reasons and the right type of personal rewards. Or you can "sign out"—admit that you're in a place that doesn't align well with your brand's values, and probably never will, which means you need to find someplace where you'll be a better fit.

Perspective here is important. We're not suggesting that your *organization* is forcing you to "sign up or sign out." We are saying, "Listen to the voice inside of you whispering, 'Sign up or sign out.'" The challenge we are ultimately presenting, however, is that it is your responsibility to act on this message—because those decisions are within your power.

Indeed, the core of the business buzzword "empowerment" is "power." And often as not, power is an inside issue, something rooted deeply inside of us, more than an outside concern. When you really look at where you are and where you want to be, don't wait for someone else to give you the power to make some changes. If you have it, use it. If you don't, either accept the realities of the situation, "vote with your feet," or use the power you do have to find a better place within your organization to build your personal brand.

Knowing how to identify your values and those of your employer can help in this regard. You now know your personal brand values. You have the tools with which to calculate the organization's. How closely do your own brand values and characteristics align with those of your employer—or how significantly do they conflict? Under those circumstances, can you sign up, or do you need to sign out? Here are a couple of real-life examples to help you see what this process looks like.

Robyn Waters

In the best of cases, when a company's brand is in sync with someone's personal brand, both come out enriched. For Karl, Robyn Waters is a perfect example. She joined Target Stores in the early '90s as a trend manager for children's clothing. Today, as part of Target's senior management team, Robyn manages the organization's entire trend department.

One of her core values is the belief that good taste and great design don't have to be expensive. Robyn believes that if more people have access to goods and services that are perceived as "in style," "with-it," "trendy," or "hip," they can choose to spend their hard-earned dollars

PERSONAL BRAND MANIFESTO

Personal Brand Dimensions for
Robyn Waters

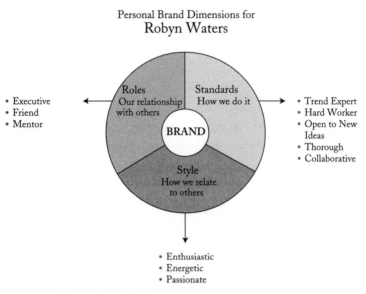

* Executive
* Friend
* Mentor

Roles
Our relationship with others

Standards
How we do it

* Trend Expert
* Hard Worker
* Open to New Ideas
* Thorough
* Collaborative

BRAND

Style
How we relate to others

* Enthusiastic
* Energetic
* Passionate

Personal Brand Platform: Open to new ideas—Brand Standard

Personal Brand Promise: "Sharing new ideas with a fresh perspective."

on things that make them feel the excitement, youthfulness, and even affluence associated with owning things that engage someone else's attention.

In some companies, that mind-set would be out of place, and someone like Robyn might constantly run into barriers. But at Target, it connects directly to the business's orientation toward trend-based value merchandising for a mass-market audience.

Target's emphasis on trend is no accident. It reflects a well-conceived business strategy. Mass-merchandise retailing is dominated by the juggernaut of Wal-Mart. To successfully compete, Target decided a number of years ago not to engage Wal-Mart on its "every-day low price" turf. Instead, drawing on its roots as part of a corporate family that includes Marshall Field's and Mervyn's, Target differentiates itself by bringing the upscale ethos of trend to the mass market. Successful trend merchandising requires a clear understanding of the emerging trends in lifestyle and fashion, and a yen for translating them for shoppers to whom price clearly is an object.

If you were Target and you were going to build a trend manager in a lab, you'd want someone with a keen sense of what is happening in the world, what is likely to happen, and how that will impact what people will buy. That person would have the high level of energy and enthusiasm necessary to stay on top of trends, a keen mind, a passion for learning more, a daring nature to explore the frontier to see what is happening, and a sharp nose for what people will buy.

Not coincidentally, those attributes describe the personal brand of Robyn Waters. She loves trend. She's tireless at it. She's passionate about it. And she has thrived at Target. The more her ideas have been accepted and used, the more enthusiastic and committed she has become. And the more her ideas have proven themselves in Target's tough competitive environment, the more confidence the organization has shown in her judgment.

"I have never loved a job as much as this one," she says. "The high-energy, innovative, forward-thinking nature of Target nourishes my love for trend and making a difference for people."

Mark Moore

The world of business has its bumps as well. For David, Mark Moore is an example of staying true to personal values in a demanding business context, even if it ultimately involves a decision to "sign out." During a successful career with Fidelity Investments, Mark rose to the level of regional vice president, building an enviable business record and achieving many of the things the business world would list under the heading of "success."

But along the way, he became unhappy with the frequent and extended absences from his family that his job often required. Deter-

PERSONAL BRAND MANIFESTO

Personal Brand Dimensions for
Mark Moore

* Institutional
Sales Rep
* Spouse
* Father
* Coach
* Mentor

Roles
Our relationship
with others

Standards
How we do it

BRAND

Style
How we relate
to others

* Industry Expert
* Client-Focused
* Always Learning
* Values Candor
* Balanced Approach
to Life

* Generous
* Encouraging
* Open
* Warm
* Dynamic

Personal Brand Platform: Balanced approach to life—Brand Standard

Personal Brand Promise: "Committed to work—passionate about family."

mined to reduce the amount of time he was spending on the road in order to have more time with his wife and young daughter, Mark responded to an overture from another financial services firm. The offer promised less travel and more nights at home. Believing the reward would be well worth the risk, he accepted and, reluctantly, left Fidelity.

Alas, modern business changes constantly. Within months of making the move, internal changes at the new company brought an unexpected challenge to Mark's resolve. The company wanted to move the Moore family to another part of the United States. The Moores didn't want to go. What to do? Sign up or sign out?

Here is where the strength of Mark's brand in his personal life and his determination to align that brand with his employer's came into play. Based on its new business needs, Mark's new employer couldn't accommodate his brand values. That didn't make it a bad company any more than Mark Moore was a bad employee for resisting the family displacement the company believed was essential to the position involved. It was just a bad fit.

The Moores could have taken the transfer and dealt with the values conflict. But a happier ending was discovered. Fidelity knew that the Mark Moores of the world are not found in abundance. He had developed an enviable reputation with clients and colleagues because of his competence, integrity, and compassion. He was well known, well remembered, and still highly respected. Hearing about his dilemma and enthusiastic about the opportunity to have him back, Fidelity was willing to discuss his return—under circumstances that took Mark's personal values into greater account.

Eventually, Fidelity offered and Mark accepted a position near his home in California—one that allows him to use his professional talents on the company's behalf while keeping his brand promise to his family: professional success built upon family values. As a result, Mark Moore is still doing work he loves, still working for a company he highly respects—yet the strength of his personal brand with his family is also at an all-time high. That's a win-win-win situation.

Thriving instead of Surviving

Most people have a lot more power than they think they have. Someone else may define what you do in the course of the day. But how you do it is in your hands. We've encountered strong personal brands in all kinds of business situations and settings—across counters in post offices, in the drive-through lanes of fast-food restaurants, in real-estate offices and hardware stores, hospital rooms and classrooms, and sitting in airline seats about as far removed from first-class as you can get while still being inside the plane.

In *The Eagle's Secret* (Dell Publishing, 1998), David used the contrast between survivors and thrivers to show the far-reaching effects even small actions and unconscious attitudes can have in our life and work. Survivors focus on work as labor, he noted. Thrivers focus on work as a laboratory: a place to learn, grow, and create. You know thrivers when you see them on the job. Clear signs reveal that they're engaged by their work, not enraged by it. Other considerations:

- Thrivers have a global perspective — they appreciate that major forces are transforming the world of work.
- Thrivers anticipate change rather than merely trying to keep up. This means continually adapting, learning, and growing.
- Thrivers seek to maximize their contribution—they are inspired by a strong sense of purpose.
- Thrivers take responsibility for their careers—they believe in self-empowerment.
- Thrivers work in harmony with others—they respect and honor differences.

And, we would add, thrivers have strong personal brands.

Every impression you make, and every impression someone else uses to build their perception of your brand, is important. Every chance you have to be passionate is a chance for you to be more of who you are. If you're in a place where you can't "sign up" and be truly committed, you are swimming against the currents or, at the very least, treading water. The potential for your life is slipping away minute by minute. Every time you compromise what you believe in, you've built the kind of brand impression you don't want.

In every part of your life, you have opportunities to grow your brand or to lose it. Never, ever, ever forget that. The point is, you're at work for eight hours a day—maybe more. You have to find a way to make those hours work *with* your brand, not against it or in spite of it. Otherwise, they truly will be "work"—something you didn't want to do yesterday, don't like to do today, and don't look forward to doing tomorrow. Life's too long to live and work that way.

Ultimately, you have to say to your organization, "Yes, I can sign up." Or, "No, I have to sign out."

And, by the way, don't underestimate the far-reaching effects of traits like cheerfulness, enthusiasm, an upbeat attitude, and simple pride in what you're doing. You know the people around you every day who feel that way, don't you? Obviously, they've "signed up." And you know the people around you who most days seem to walk under their own private cloud. Too bad they haven't "signed out," isn't it?

Which ones do customers, internal or external, respond to, and which ones leave them wishing they'd gone somewhere else?

Which ones do *you* like being with, and which ones are you prone to avoid making eye contact with?

What do those impressions say about the personal brands involved?

And if you feel that way, what makes you think the people around you can't—and don't—make the same kind of assessments about you?

It's your brand. It's your life. Sign up or sign out.

9 The Courage to Live Your Brand

The personal brand you create will become a dynamic presence in your life. But to remain strong, it must be renewed every day. It must become a part of everything you do.

On some days, those objectives will be easy to achieve. On other days, you'll face situations that will challenge your ability to stand by the sense of purpose, vision, and values you've chosen to center your life on. You'll also encounter times when your brand promise will be severely challenged.

You'll face times when your brand building seems to be on hold—when life tries to lull you into a state of complacency, even apathy. Whether the seas are rough or calm, your brand needs to be strong enough to ride out the waves and keep moving in the direction you've chosen.

We want to leave you with one last concept from the brand-builder's dictionary—**brand moments**. Those are the times when your unique combination of roles, standards, and style will be put to the test—when you'll have a chance to be found distinctively and consistently relevant to someone else. In those moments, your brand will shine. Or fade.

Brand moments are opportunities to dramatize the important dimensions of your brand in ways that add memorable clarity to the way you make and keep promises and commitments. Often these moments will be encountered unexpectedly, but you can still prepare for them in advance. Think about the possible scenarios in which your brand may be tested. Where are they likely to come from? How should your brand respond to remain true to your values and its roles, standards, and style? Under what circumstances will you willingly take on greater risk or responsibility? How far "above and beyond" are you prepared to go if new conditions create an opportunity for an out-of-the-ordinary response?

The essence of living a strong personal brand is recognizing and managing those moments—however important or ordinary they may appear—on behalf of your brand's immediate and long-term interests. Just as a business brand needs champions, so, too, does your personal brand need you to consciously build the relationships through which you and your brand will thrive and succeed.

Some days, that will be a simple matter of doing what comes naturally within the context of those relationships. And you'll find in those moments that you're not alone: When you have a strong brand, you'll attract allies. The people to whom your brand matters will be drawn to it. They'll support it. They'll fight for it. And you.

Other days, you'll be called upon to go above and beyond what you usually bring to the relationship. Your values will be put under the microscope. Your commitment—to yourself, to your brand, and to the people who depend on you and matter to you—will be tested.

Everyday life presents people with constant opportunities to refine their brands in the crucible of simple acts. To add to the gossip or defend a friend (or someone who isn't a friend). To wallow in the worst of a situation or look for the best in it. To take the easy way out or stand by their brand. To indulge a bad habit or reinforce a good one. To take a little more than they need or give a little more than is required.

The continual—and ultimately life-defining—tests of the values that underlie your brand can arise out of just these kinds of simple, everyday dilemmas. To get credit for your beliefs means dealing with the ordinary as well as the extraordinary, rising to the challenges as well as keeping on an even keel, acting forthrightly in situations you control, and reacting capably in situations you don't control.

Brand moments offer tremendous potential to define, strengthen, and communicate your brand and its values. You can either dread these moments for the challenges they represent or look ahead to them as the opportunities they are. You can even practice responses for how you'll handle them. Either way, when the pressure's on—and the spotlight is on you—you'll face a moment of truth for the brand you want to be.

Here are ten ways to prepare yourself for the important moments when your personal brand is put to the test.

1. Develop and refine your personal brand manifesto. The objective of building a strong personal brand is to get credit for who you are and what you believe. The process can be enhanced considerably if you give yourself time to think through the implications of that quest and identify the resources you bring to it before the proverbial "last minute."

That's not as easy as it may sound. Most of us have so many demands on our time and attention, we seldom take a break for reflection. We're running from the instant we roll out of bed to start the day to the time we flop back in, totally exhausted, at day's end. It's not surprising that we don't make time for some systematic personal assessment. Yet without some periodic self-maintenance, even what we might consider our most cherished beliefs can get a little fuzzy around the edges.

Throughout this book, we've scattered detailed snapshots of the brand roles, standards, and style of people we've used as exemplars of strong personal brands. From their stories and these charts, you'll see the essential pieces of a brand puzzle emerging. We encourage you to use these pieces with the Personal Brand Dimensions Model template to develop your own personal brand manifesto. What roles are you called on to supply in the relationships that matter in your life? What standards can you build on? What style characteristics help fill in the subtle dimensions of your brand?

2. Be "brand proud."   If you want to be perceived as a strong personal brand, you have to decide what you stand for, and then you have to be that to the nth degree. You have to work from a firm values platform, not shifting sand. When your vision and values are put to the test, your roles, standards, and style need to align and capably represent the authentic you.

The values profile in Appendix I is one important resource to draw on. Revisit it periodically and watch for signs of both consistency and change. Use the "top seven" process to track your strengths and the shifting priorities others present through the brand relationships in your life. Then consciously make these values a part of your character.

Your values must be valuable to *you*, so stand up for them. You can't "kind of, sort of, most of the time" believe in your values or act from them only periodically when the conditions seem right. You have to live those values consistently, courageously, even dramatically, on a day-to-day basis. How else can the people who know you and depend on you trust that they can count on you, no matter how convenient or inconvenient the moment?

3. Audit your brand promises.   From your personal brand manifesto and your detailed understanding of your bedrock values, you should find it increasingly easy and natural to crystallize the essence of what you bring to the important relationships in your life. Develop a compelling, passionate, and motivating brand promise, and use it as the focal point of your actions.

Continually revisit and refine your promise in the light of new experiences and insights. Listen carefully to what people say, and watch what they do in response to your efforts. If you're achieving the desired effect, what can you learn from this success to increase the odds of building even greater value with each new contact? If you're coming up a little short, what do you need to do to close the distance between where you are and where you want to be?

Take private time to reflect. Get feedback from others. Don't guess about the status of important relationships. Boil your intentions down to a promise you will keep, and then make sure you're keeping it.

4. Be authentic.   Strong personal brands are built by making conscious, conscientious choices based on what you truly stand for. And once those choices are made, you have to be willing to stand up for them when the world doesn't immediately line up and sing your praises. Really great brands, business or personal, reflect the values and convictions of their originators as demonstrated over time.

You don't get the reputation of a FedEx unless and until you really do act on an unrelenting commitment to deliver. You don't attract the clientele of a Ritz-Carlton unless and until you really do treat your own people and your guests like ladies and gentlemen, not some unknown, unimportant traveler in Room 410.

Good or bad, the parents, teachers, bosses, colleagues, friends, and—if you're lucky—lovers who have shaped the course of your life have shown you a connection between their actions and their soul. The people who value their relationships with you have the same feeling about you, the same kind of emotional bond. It's not an easy bond to create. But the payoff for the effort can be profoundly worthwhile.

5. Make sure the signals you send convey relevance to others.   Being a strong personal brand *absolutely* requires sensitivity to the needs of other people. Brands are relationships. Your brand image exists in someone else's head. You don't create it in a vacuum. To create a clear image of being distinctive, relevant, and consistent in response to someone else's needs means establishing a clear channel for communications—then sending out something that truly meets those needs.

For many people, finding a balance between "me" and "we" can be a troubling issue in personal brand management. You may have a strong sense of the person you want to be, the signal you want to send. But you may feel anything from a vague discontent to an outright unhappiness because the connections you expect as a result aren't in place, or aren't holding up over time, or aren't validating the sense of value you believe you represent.

Check the frequencies. Could your brand messages and behaviors lack enough passion and energy to be heard? Or could they be indistinguishable from all the other "noise" in the spectrum of daily life? Is your message distinctive? Are your values in harmony with your roles, standards, and style? Are you "on the air" all the time, or just broadcasting periodically—and not on a regular schedule?

Fine-tune the signals you're sending and you may find that your brand begins to connect in the way that you want it to.

6. Consistency. Consistency. Consistency. If you're acting from a coherent belief system, people should see consistency in your actions and learn to value you accordingly. And although they don't know *why* you do what you do, they will interpret your actions as a projection of a consistent belief and value system, and credit you in that context.

In business, it's axiomatic that "everything counts" for the customer. For your brand, as well, everything counts. Pay attention to the consistency of the impressions you make. Keep your head in the game. Great brand relationships aren't built on one-time encounters. They are created, nurtured, and solidified by conscious long-term effort in which even apparently inconsequential details get attention and are managed consistently toward a desired objective.

Pay attention to what you do and how you do it. What's "normal" for you in the relationships you value? Why is that normal behavior both distinctive and relevant to someone else? What can you do to improve those aspects of your behavior while enhancing your consistency? When you find the right places to be, map them out and develop them into strong, healthy environments — for everyone involved.

7. Make sure your package reflects your contents.   Your brand is a perception stored in someone else's mind. This means that everything they see, hear, sense, feel—even wonder about—is added to the composite picture they carry around with your name under it. If you could see that picture, would you recognize yourself?

People learn with their eyes much faster, and with much more lasting impact, than they do with their ears. Researchers find that well over half the impact we have on another person comes not from our words but from our tone of voice and, more importantly, our body language and the other elements that make up our visual package.

How you look and the way you talk can be great tools for establishing a strong personal brand. Be personal brand–savvy with the way you look and the way you communicate. As an example, notice how impeccably any U.S. Marine is dressed and put together. That "starched" look and demeanor goes a long way to reinforce the discipline that is the core component of their brand platform. By comparison, imagine Albert Einstein, a wrinkled, disheveled-looking, eccentric genius. His look reinforced the perception that all his energy was being focused on making the next theoretical breakthrough in physics; he didn't have time to comb his hair or make sure his shirt fit. His presentation certainly reinforced his brand platform of intelligence.

Your "package" should be an accurate reflection of what's inside: make sure the impressions you're creating are the ones you want to be creating. Set an impeccable standard for everything that adds up to how others perceive you. Your smile, your facial expressions, your posture, the way you use your hands and your eyes, the words you choose, your tone of voice, how you're dressed, and the environment in which someone finds you—all contribute to your brand identity.

8. Great brands are known by the company they keep. As you become clearer about your values and the way you want them to connect to others, you will gain a useful standard for evaluating the people in your life. Being a strong brand means people recognize that certain values are essential to you being yourself. Your friends—your true friends—are attracted by those values. They don't try to make you into something you're not. They see you for what you are, and they value you because what you are is relevant to their lives. That cohesion builds a kind of community far more powerful than anything defined by a zip code.

So make conscious choices about the significant (and insignificant) others in your life. Surround yourself with a supportive community of friends and associates who share the vision and values important to your brand.

This won't be as hard as you might think. Strong personal brands, just like strong business brands, attract people with similar beliefs. People really do know it (whatever "it" is) when they see it, and they move closer or farther away accordingly. When you're clear about who you are and what you will do on someone else's behalf, people will either accept that or look for a more relevant connection somewhere else. Those who value the things in which you are strong will want to associate with you. Those who don't, won't.

You can consciously guide that continuing selection process. In the light of brand relationships, take a good look at the people you habitually surround yourself with. Brands get energy from the like-minded brands around them. They can lose energy when they're surrounded by incompatible brands. Evaluate your relationships. Are the personal brands in your life nourishing your brand or stunting its growth?

9. Synchronize your brand with your employer's.   One axiom of coaching is to put people in positions where they can succeed. The baseball manager who sends the light-hitting utility infielder out to bat cleanup is as much to blame as anyone else when the hapless player strikes out with the bases loaded. The ballet producer who pushes the ninth swan from the left to center stage and expects a prima ballerina performance worthy of the Bolshoi needs to shoulder much of the responsibility when the audience starts shifting uncomfortably in their seats.

The same holds true for you and your brand, but you're both the performer and the coach. Give yourself a fighting chance. Put yourself in positions where you can succeed. Take yourself out of situations where you are doomed to fail—or worse, may have to compromise your values to get by. Knowing your values, understanding your strengths and weaknesses, and polishing your relationship skills avail you nothing if you don't take the initiative to make sure you're the right person in the right place.

None of us live in a perfect world. Odds are we never will. A lot of the strong personal brands around you are based on values you don't share. We all have to accept that the people attached to brands and values we disagree with may be fully content that those brands reflect their inner souls. The workplace is one arena in which those conflicts tend to surface.

If your employer doesn't share your values, you can stay and struggle—and likely get beaten down from your unappreciated efforts. Or you can go to work for people who appreciate the values you bring to work with you and will align them with their own for everyone's greater success.

Find out what your employer's—or boss's—brand values are and compare them to your own. Are there obvious linkages? Inevitable conflicts? Immediate compatibilities? Major gulfs? Against this backdrop, how can you make your own brand values distinctive and relevant in a consistent way?

10. Start counting relationships as part of your asset base. We believe real success, for a life as well as a brand, is defined in terms of relationships. What really enriches everyone's lives are the people who love them, like them, trust them, rely on them, enjoy being with them, or even simply tolerate them.

There's a huge difference between building a web of mutually rewarding relationships and storing a file of names in a personal digital assistant or address book. To build a strong and viable relationship with someone calls for a form of selflessness that even mature people must occasionally struggle to attain.

If you decide who you are and the kinds of relationships that are important to you, and then act consistently on that vision and those values, you are being fundamentally true to yourself. And if you are fundamentally true to yourself, you will discover a treasure trove of riches and accomplishment.

The Art and Soul of a Personal Brand

We believe—and we hope we've shown you—that a strong personal brand goes much deeper than the superficial veneer of a slick image. Brands are relationships. They reflect values.

What happens now is entirely up to you. This was never intended to be a feel-good book. It is intended to be a do-good book. We can't tell you what's right for you in any given situation. Only you can determine that. But the key is to make those determinations not on the basis of your own needs alone but in the context of the connections you want to build with others.

Creating and living a strong personal brand is for others, not just for yourself. It's one of the best investments you'll ever make. The world needs strong brands. It respects them. It relies on them. If you can be one, we'll all be the richer for it.

Appendix I: Brand Values Profile

Step One: Place a check mark in the appropriate column to indicate its relative importance to you. Rate all values on the list. Use the "Other" spaces to add values important to you but not included on this list.

Value Description	Not important	Somewhat important	Very important
Achievement (results, tasks completed)			
Adventure (new experiences, challenge, excitement)			
Artistic Expression (drama, painting, literature)			
Balance (proper attention to each area of life)			
Competition (desire to win, to take risks)			
Contribution (desire to make a difference, to give)			
Control (desire to be in charge, sense of order)			
Cooperation (teamwork, working with others)			
Creativity (new ideas, innovation, experimenting)			
Economic Security (freedom from financial worries)			
Fairness (equal chance, equal hearing for all)			
Fame (desire to be well-known, recognized)			
Family Happiness (desire to get along, respect, harmony)			
Friendship (intimacy, caring, support)			
Generosity (desire to give time or money readily)			
Health (physical fitness, energy, no disease)			
Independence (self-reliance, freedom from controls)			
Influence (desire to shape ideas, people, processes)			
Inner Harmony (desire to be at peace with oneself)			
Integrity (honesty, sincerity, consistent demonstration of your values)			
Learning (growth, knowledge, understanding)			
Loyalty (duty, allegiance, respect)			
Nature (care for and appreciation of the environment)			
Order (organization, conformity, stability)			
Personal Development (improvement, reach potential)			
Pleasure (enjoyment, fun, happiness)			
Power (authority, influence over people and/or situations)			

(continued)

Value Description	Not important	Somewhat important	Very important
Prestige (visible success, rank, status)			
Quality (excellence, high standards, minimal errors)			
Recognition (respect, acknowledgment, applause)			
Responsibility (desire to be accountable, trustworthy, mature)			
Security (desire to feel safe about things, surroundings)			
Service (desire to assist others, to improve society)			
Self Respect (pride in self, feeling worthy)			
Spirituality (belief or interest in a higher power or God)			
Stability (continuity, predictability)			
Tolerance (openness to others, their views and values)			
Tradition (treasuring the past, customs)			
Variety (diversity of activities and experiences)			
Wealth (material prosperity, affluence, abundance)			
Wisdom (desire to understand life, to exercise sound judgment)			
Other:			
Other:			

Step Two: After checking the relative importance of all the values, look at those you checked as being "very important." Your goal for this survey is to refine your list of very important values to the seven you consider most important. Go back through the list and choose the seven values that are most important to you. Record these seven values in any order on the lines below.

Top 7 "Very Important" Values

1. _____

2. _____

3. _____

4. _____

5. _____

6. _____

7. _____

Appendix II: Personal Brand Manifestos

We have included here a blank Personal Brand Manifesto form for your use, as well as all of the Personal Brand Manifestos we used as personal brand examples in the book.

PERSONAL BRAND MANIFESTO

Personal Brand Dimensions for

_____

Personal Brand Platform: _____

Personal Brand Promise: _____

PERSONAL BRAND MANIFESTO

Personal Brand Dimensions for
Chip Bell

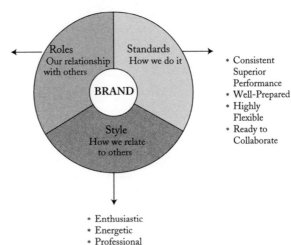

* Speaker
* Writer
* Father
* Husband

Roles — Our relationship with others

Standards — How we do it

BRAND

Style — How we relate to others

* Consistent Superior Performance
* Well-Prepared
* Highly Flexible
* Ready to Collaborate

* Enthusiastic
* Energetic
* Professional

Personal Brand Platform: Enthusiastic—Brand Style

Personal Brand Promise: "Enthusiasm that will make your day."

PERSONAL BRAND MANIFESTO

Personal Brand Dimensions for
David Dunn

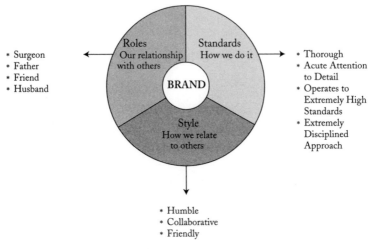

* Surgeon
* Father
* Friend
* Husband

* Thorough
* Acute Attention to Detail
* Operates to Extremely High Standards
* Extremely Disciplined Approach

* Humble
* Collaborative
* Friendly

Personal Brand Platform: Disciplined approach—Brand Standard

Personal Brand Promise: "The discipline to achieve world-class results."

PERSONAL BRAND MANIFESTO

Personal Brand Dimensions for
Jacque Rast

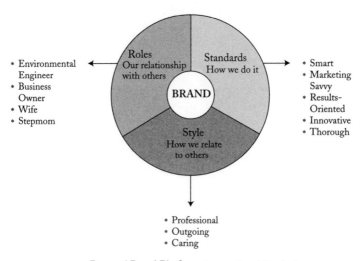

* Environmental
  Engineer
* Business
  Owner
* Wife
* Stepmom

* Smart
* Marketing
  Savvy
* Results-
  Oriented
* Innovative
* Thorough

* Professional
* Outgoing
* Caring

Personal Brand Platform: Smart—Brand Standard

Personal Brand Promise: "Smart ideas put into action."

PERSONAL BRAND MANIFESTO

Personal Brand Dimensions for
James Scothorn

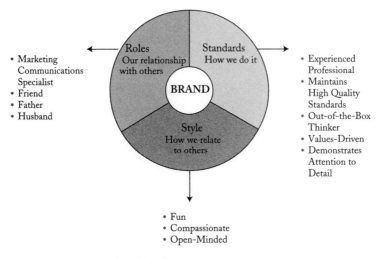

* Marketing
  Communications
  Specialist
* Friend
* Father
* Husband

* Experienced
  Professional
* Maintains
  High Quality
  Standards
* Out-of-the-Box
  Thinker
* Values-Driven
* Demonstrates
  Attention to
  Detail

* Fun
* Compassionate
* Open-Minded

Personal Brand Platform: Values-driven—Brand Standard

Personal Brand Promise: "Do it right for the right reasons."

PERSONAL BRAND MANIFESTO

Personal Brand Dimensions for
Jeannie Seeley-Smith

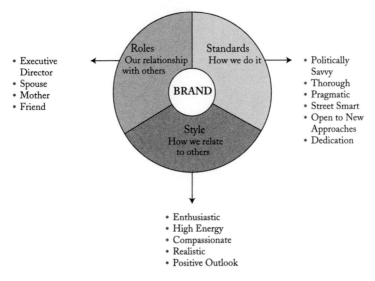

* Executive
  Director
* Spouse
* Mother
* Friend

* Politically
  Savvy
* Thorough
* Pragmatic
* Street Smart
* Open to New
  Approaches
* Dedication

* Enthusiastic
* High Energy
* Compassionate
* Realistic
* Positive Outlook

Personal Brand Platform: Compassionate—Brand Style

Personal Brand Promise: "The insight to guide, the compassion to inspire."

PERSONAL BRAND MANIFESTO

Personal Brand Dimensions for
Mark Moore

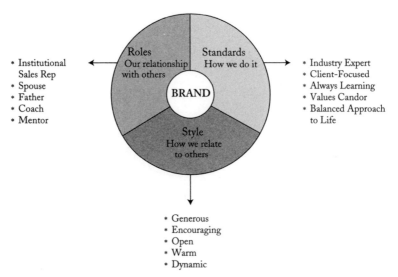

* Institutional
  Sales Rep
* Spouse
* Father
* Coach
* Mentor

* Industry Expert
* Client-Focused
* Always Learning
* Values Candor
* Balanced Approach
  to Life

* Generous
* Encouraging
* Open
* Warm
* Dynamic

Personal Brand Platform: Balanced approach to life—Brand Standard

Personal Brand Promise: "Committed to work—passionate about family."

PERSONAL BRAND MANIFESTO

Personal Brand Dimensions for
Robyn Waters

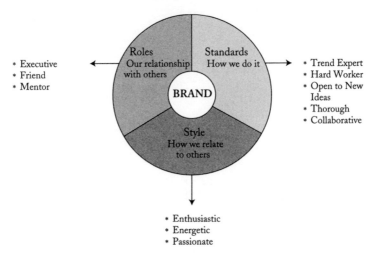

* Executive
* Friend
* Mentor

Roles Our relationship with others

Standards How we do it

BRAND

Style How we relate to others

* Trend Expert
* Hard Worker
* Open to New Ideas
* Thorough
* Collaborative

* Enthusiastic
* Energetic
* Passionate

Personal Brand Platform: Open to new ideas—Brand Standard

Personal Brand Promise: "Sharing new ideas with a fresh perspective."

Appendix III: Reading List

Berry, Leonard L. *Discovering the Soul of Service: The Nine Drivers of Sustainable Business Success* (New York: The Free Press). 1999

Leider, Richard. *Repacking Your Bags: Lighten Your Load for the Rest of Your Life* (San Francisco: Berrett-Koehler Publishers). 1996.

———. *Whistle While You Work: Heeding Your Life's Calling* (San Francisco: Berrett-Koehler Publishers). 2001.

McNally, David. *The Eagle's Secret: Success Strategies for Thriving at Work and in Life* (New York: Delacorte Press). 1999.

Miller, James B., and Paul B. Brown. *The Corporate Coach* (New York: HarperBusiness). 1994.

Index

A

Aaker, Jennifer, 61, 62
Alcoa, 104
Angelou, Maya, 17
Appearance, personal, 123–24
Applebee's, 39
Aspiration, 16
Audience, intended, 13, 38–39
Authenticity
  courage and, 48
  definition of, 47
  impact of, 10
  in relationships, 47, 121
  signposts on the road to, 48–54

B

Bell, Chip (example)
  personal brand dimensions for, 31–32, 35, 36, 37
  personal brand manifesto for, 132
  personal brand promise for, 78
  as strong personal brand, 9–10
Berry, Len, 90
Beyond Marketing Thought, 25

Body language, 123–24
Brand alignment, 74. See also Employer's brand
Brand equity, 26, 43, 84–85
Brand ladders, 19–21
Brand loyalty, 106
Brand measurement, 60, 91–97
Brand moments, 117–19
Brand platforms, 60, 72, 77–78
Brand promises
  auditing, 120–21
  brand platform and, 77–78
  creating, 77–78
  definition of, 49, 60, 74
  examples of, 76, 78, 82–83
  keeping, 74–77
  to spouses and life partners, 83–84
  statement of, 74, 108
  targeting, 78–80
  at work, 80–83
Brands. See also Business brands; Personal brands
  appropriate, 8–9
  books on, 25

Brands *(continued)*
consistency and, 13, 17, 88,
122–23
definition of, 4
distinctiveness of, 13
lasting, 89–90
personality traits of, 61–62
as relationships, 2–3, 4–5, 46, 76
relevance and, 13
roles and, 26
standards and, 26, 68–70
strong, 6–7, 8, 13, 69, 70
style and, 26
ubiquity of, 7
Brand strategy
in business, 106
names for, 107
personal, 58
of your employer, 107–8
Broken window syndrome, 70–71
Business brands
alignment of, 74
building, 62, 67
competencies and, 26, 28,
30–31, 38
consistency and, 17
definition of, 1–2, 4
intended audience for, 13
measuring, 91–92, 95–96
quality and, 7
standards and, 26
strong, 6–7, 8, 13, 54, 67, 68
style and, 26
success and, 5
ubiquity of, 7
values and, 54

C

Cargill, 103–4
Children, vision of, 51–52
Chili's, 39
Clarity, 68–70
Coca-Cola, 7
Commitment, 14, 73–74
Competencies
business brands and, 26, 28,
30–31, 38
common meaning of, 28
roles vs., 27, 28, 29
standards and, 34
Complaints, 95–96, 100
Consistency
business brands and, 17
courage and, 24
lack of, 18, 19, 94
personal brands and, 16–18,
23–24, 66–67, 122–23
in relationships, 17–18
Corporate identity strategy. See
Brand strategy
Courage
to be authentic, 47–48
to be consistent, 24
to live your brand, 117–28
Creation, 51

D

Dickinson, Emily, 47
Distinctiveness, 13, 14–15, 23–24
Domino's, 69
Dunn, David (example)
personal brand dimensions for,
41–42

personal brand manifesto for, 133

E

Einstein, Albert, 123
Emotions
  personal brands and, 61–62
  relationships and, 7–8, 11, 62
  staying power of, 11
  style and, 35–36
Employer's brand. See also Work
  bad fit with, 112–14, 116
  core values and, 108
  defining, 107–9
  examples of, 103–4, 110–14
  linking with, 101–3, 106–9,
    110–12, 115–16, 125–26
Expectations
  clarity in, 68–70
  exceeding, 11

F

FedEx, 43, 54, 68, 76, 78–79, 80,
  88, 104, 121
Fidelity Investments, 112–14
The Firm, 89
Fox, Terry, 18–19
Friendship, 85–86, 124–25

G

Gotti, John, 22–23
Grisham, John, 89
Guidelines, 97–98

H

Habitat for Humanity, 104

I

Inconsistency, 18, 19, 94

L

Leider, Dick, 52
Life partners, brand promise to,
  83–84
Limbaugh, Rush, 17

M

Marriott, 68
Marshall Field's, 111
McDonald's, 17, 30, 38, 43, 68
Medtronic, 104
Meiss Education Institute, 55
Mervyn's, 111
Miller, Jim, 98
Mindfulness, 73
Mistakes, 11, 88
Moore, Mark (example)
  employer's brand and, 112–14
  personal brand manifesto for,
    113, 137
Morality, 22–23
Motel 6, 17, 68

N

Nader, Ralph, 17

P

Parent-child relationship, 29–30,
  84–85
Passion, 67
Perceptions
  key, 28
  reality vs., 1, 11, 28, 91

Personal Brand Dimensions
    Model, 25–27
    examples of, 31–32, 35, 36, 37,
        39–43, 66
    interlocking nature of, 37–38, 79
    roles in, 26, 30–32, 63
    standards in, 26, 27, 32–35,
        63–64
    style in, 26, 27, 35–37, 65
    using, 60, 62–67, 71–72, 119–20
Personal brand manifestos. See
    also Brand strategy
    blank form for, 131
    developing and refining, 119–20
    elements of, 60
    examples of, 132–38
Personal brand platforms. See
    Brand platforms
Personal brand promises. See
    Brand promises
Personal brands
    being proud of, 120
    benefit to you of, 12
    "broken windows" for, 70–71
    building, 60, 61–62, 73–74
    commitment to, 14, 73–74
    communicating your, 121–22
    consistency and, 16–18, 23–24,
        66–67, 122–23
    courage and, 24
    definition of, 2–3, 4
    differences in, 42–43
    distinctiveness of, 14–15, 23–24
    emotions and, 61–62
    examples of, 9–10, 132–38
    intended audience for, 13
    managing, 60, 97–100

    measuring, 60, 92–94, 96–97
    morality and, 22–23
    perceptions of, 6
    personal appearance and, 123–24
    purpose and, 49–51
    random, 71
    as relationships, 2–3, 4–5,
        121–22
    relevance and, 15–16, 21–22,
        23–24, 67
    roles and, 26, 30–32, 63, 67
    standards and, 27, 33–35, 63–64,
        66–67
    strong, 6–7, 8, 13, 14–18, 22–23,
        118, 126–27
    style and, 26, 27, 32–35, 63–64,
        66–67
    synchronizing with employer's
        brand, 101–3, 110–12,
        125–26
    tests of, 118–19
    values and, 3, 15, 23, 54, 66
    vision and, 51–53
Personal Brand Values Profile,
    55–58, 129–30
Personal Values Profile, 55
Perspectives, 63, 65
Positioning strategy. See Brand
    strategy
Positive attitude, 100
Public figures, 17
Purpose, importance of, 49–51

Q
Quality, importance of, 7

R

Rast, Jacque (example)
  personal brand manifesto for, 83, 134
  personal brand promise for, 78, 81–83
Reagan, Ronald, 17
Reality vs. perception, 1, 11, 28, 91
Recognition, 99–100
Relationships
  authenticity in, 47
  brand promises and, 80, 83–86
  brands as, 2–3, 4–5, 46, 76, 121–22
  clarity in, 22
  consistency in, 17–18
  emotions and, 7–8, 11, 62
  evaluating, 124–25
  evolving, 19–20, 21, 27
  lasting, 89–90
  most important, 8, 80
  parent-child, 29–30, 84–85
  purpose and, 50–51
  roles in, 27, 29–30
  standards in, 27, 29–30
  style in, 27, 29–30
  success and, 4–5, 50, 126
  supporting your personal brand, 124–25
  values and, 54
Relevance, 13, 15–16, 21–22, 23–24, 67
Rewards, 99–100
Ritz-Carlton, 17, 43, 68, 121
Roles
  areas using your, 63
  competencies vs., 27, 28, 29
  in the Personal Brand Dimensions Model, 26, 30–32, 63
  in relationships, 27, 29–30
  varying nature of, 67

S

Scothorn, James (example)
  personal brand dimensions for, 39–41
  personal brand manifesto for, 135
  personal brand promise for, 78
Seely-Smith, Jeannie (example)
  personal brand dimensions for, 62–65, 66
  personal brand manifesto for, 136
  personal brand platform for, 77
  personal brand promise for, 78
Special events, 99
Spouses, brand promise to, 83–84
Standards
  clarity and, 68–70
  common meaning of, 28
  competencies and, 34
  examining your, 63–64
  in the Personal Brand Dimensions Model, 26, 27, 32–35, 63–64
  in relationships, 27, 29–30
Steinem, Gloria, 17
Style
  common meaning of, 28
  defining your, 65

Style *(continued)*
in the Personal Brand
Dimensions Model, 26, 27,
35–37, 65
in relationships, 27, 29–30
Success
defining, 73
importance of relationships to,
4–5, 50, 126
personal, 5
values and, 45–46
Survivors, 115

T

Talisman Partners, 82
Target Stores, 110–12
Terry Fox Foundation, 19
"Thinking in reverse," 16
Thrivers, 115
Training, 98–99
Transactions, 90–91
Trust, 18, 50

U

UPS, 54, 68, 88
U.S. Postal Service, 88

V

Values
business brands and, 54
connecting personal brand to, 3,
15, 23, 54, 72
definition of, 14
employer's core, 108
examining your, 63–64
identifying your, 54–58, 129–30
importance of, 45, 55
relationships and, 54
standing up for your, 120
success and, 45–46
tests of, 105–6, 118–19
Vision, importance of, 51–53
Voice, tone of, 123–24

W

Wal-Mart, 111
Waters, Robyn (example)
employer's brand and, 110–12
personal brand manifesto for,
111, 138
Wendy's, 30, 38
Word-of-mouth, 96–97
Work. See also Employer's brand
brand promises at, 80–83
fulfillment at, 103–4
irritating people at, 106

David McNally has enjoyed an extensive international business career, including assignments in South Africa, Europe, and the South Pacific. He is the producer of the award-winning film *The Power of Purpose* and the author of two best-selling books, *Even Eagles Need a Push: Learning to Soar in a Changing World* and *The Eagle's Secret: Success Strategies for Thriving at Work and in Life*. Companies such as Fidelity Investments, Pfizer, Merrill Lynch, Pulte Homes, and American Express have embraced David's work as a key component in preparing their employees for an ever more competitive and complex future. He is described by his audiences as a dynamic and captivating presenter, a leading Washington, D.C., speakers bureau says: "We regard David McNally as one of the top fifty speakers in the world today."

Contact information: Trans-Form Corporation, 10249 Yellow Circle Drive, Suite 225, Minnetonka, MN 55343. Telephone: (952) 930-9208; Fax: (952) 930-9216; Email: info@davidmcnally.com; Website: www.davidmcnally.com

Karl D. Speak is a consultant who delivers powerful insights and practical advice on brand-management issues. His activities on behalf of Beyond Marketing Thought, the company he founded in 1984, are at the foundation of his experience and knowledge.

Karl has implemented his contemporary approach to brand management with a wide range of corporate clients, such as Allina Health System, United Health-care, Honeywell, Cargill, Marshall Field's, American Airlines, Federal Express, ING, Quest, IBM, U.S. Bancorp, Pillsbury Company, AT&T, Motorola, Skandia, Lutheran Brotherhood, Scotts Company, Stanley Tool Works, *Wall Street Journal,* 3M, Sony, and Target Stores.

An accomplished presenter, Karl speaks to many different types of audiences around the world. His energetic style and wide-reaching knowledge of brand management make him a favorite speaker with executive teams. Karl has trained hundreds of marketing profession-als in corporate training seminars. He also teaches brand management at the University of Minnesota, College of St. Thomas, and the University of Westminster.

Contact information: Beyond Marketing Thought, 510 First Avenue North, Suite 605, Minneapolis, MN 55403. Telephone: (612) 338-5009; Fax: (612) 338-4714; Email: info@brandnetwork.com

Berrett-Koehler Publishers

Berrett-Koehler is an independent publisher of books and other publications at the leading edge of new thinking and innovative practice on work, business, management, leadership, stewardship, career development, human resources, entrepreneurship, and global sustainability.

Since the company's founding in 1992, we have been committed to creating a world that works for all by publishing books that help us to integrate our values with our work and work lives, and to create more humane and effective organizations.

We have chosen to focus on the areas of work, business, and organizations, because these are central elements in many people's lives today. Furthermore, the work world is going through tumultuous changes, from the decline of job security to the rise of new structures for organizing people and work. We believe that change is needed at all levels—individual, organizational, community, and global—and our publications address each of these levels.

To find out about our new books,
special offers,
free excerpts,
and much more,
subscribe to our free monthly eNewsletter at

www.bkconnection.com

Spread the word!

Berrett-Koehler books and audios are available at quantity discounts for orders of 10 or more copies.

Be Your Own Brand
A Breakthrough Formula for Standing Our from the Crowd
David McNally and Karl D. Speak

Paperback, 160 pages
ISBN 1-57675-272-0
Item #52720-415
$14.95

To find out about discounts on orders of 10 or more copies for individuals, corporations, institutions, and organizations, please call us toll-free at (800) 929-2929.

To find out about our discount programs for resellers, please contact our Special Sales department at (415) 288-0260; Fax: (415) 362-2512. Or email us at bkpub@bkpub.com.

Subscribe to our free e-newsletter!
To find out about what's happening at Berrett-Koehler and to receive announcements of our new books, special offers, free excerpts, and much more, subscribe to our free monthly e-newsletter at www.bkconnection.com.

Berrett-Koehler Publishers
PO Box 565, Williston, VT 05495-9900
Call toll-free! **800-929-2929** 7 am-9 pm Eastern Standard Time
Or fax your order to 802-864-7627
For fastest service order online: **www.bkconnection.com**